Feed Me Well, Ilona

Goldie M. Down

Pacific Press Publishing Association
Boise, Idaho
Montemorelos, Nuevo Leon, Mexico
Oshawa, Ontario, Canada

Designed by Tim Larson
Cover art by Sue Rother

Copyright © 1985 by
Pacific Press Publishing Association
Printed in United States of America
All Rights Reserved

Library of Congress Cataloging in Publication Data

Down, Goldie M.
  Feed me well, Ilona.

  (Destiny II)
  1. Nagy, Gyula, 1926-   . 2. Balog, Ilona. 3. Seventh-day Advent-
ists—Australia—Biography. I. Title.
BX6191.D678   1985   286.7'32'0922 [B]   84-14833

ISBN 0-8163-0575-7

85 86 87 88 89 ● 6 5 4 3 2 1

Dedication

To Glenda and John Quin, and to the countless other selfless adults who plant seeds of truth in the mind of a child.

Contents

Gyula Nagy

Papa Nagy, a shoemaker and cobbler and as poor as the proverbial church mouse, toiled long hours at his workshop in Harsny
village, marking and cutting the leather and painstakingly sewing
the pieces into fashionable thigh boots, which he sold at nearby
country fairs. But either Papa was a slow worker or a poor busi-
nessman, because the price he received for the boots scarcely
covered the cost of the leather; certainly the tiny profit that he
made did little to boost the family finances.

Mama Nagy did her bit. She brought home piecework sewing
from an underwear factory, and the kitchen seemed always filled
with the whirring of her hand-powered sewing machine while the
scattered bits and pieces of undergarments took shape under her
busy fingers.

Not that she had much time for sewing, poor woman, not with a
husband and three small children to cook and wash and iron and
clean for. Istvan, the eldest son, had not reached three years and
Andras was but fifteen months old when little Gyula arrived. Two
years later Laszlo came on the scene and after him, Mariska, fortunately, completed the family.

Mama Nagy's three younger sisters had married men of means,
but Mama was the poor relation. However, being the oldest in the
family, she had inherited the ancestral home.

The two-bedroom house with a large kitchen had the added bo-
nus of a medium-size backyard, where straggling grapevines and a
handful of plum and pear trees withstood determined childish
onslaughts. A rickety chicken run confined a flock of cackling

hens that did their brave best to keep the family supplied with eggs.

In spring and summer the growing family helped Mama tend the tiny vegetable patch that yielded beets, turnips, and cabbages— sometimes enough cabbages to make into sauerkraut and store in the cellar against winter shortages.

Sometimes there was scarcely enough food to satisfy seven hungry stomachs, nor sufficient warm garments to clothe five growing children, and certainly never enough money to purchase one twentieth of the items the family *needed,* to say nothing of their wants.

When little Gyula reached the age of two he fell ill. His face flushed with fever and his body felt hot to touch, even though he shivered as if he were cold. He coughed often and moaned with every painful, wheezing breath. Mama Nagy put him to bed and tried all the usual remedies for colds and influenza: she tied a eucalyptus-soaked rag around his neck and applied a mustard plaster to his chest. She mixed lemon and honey into a soothing syrup for his cough.

But nothing did any good. Little Gyula cried out and tossed in delirium, and Mama in desperation wrung her hands as she talked to Papa, "Whether we can afford to pay him or not, we must call a doctor."

Papa ran as if he had wings on his feet. Papa was fond of his wife and family, and he could not bear to think of losing one of them.

The doctor came. He asked a few questions, took the little boy's temperature, and listened to his wheezing chest. Then he stood back and shook his head.

"He has pneumonia. There's not a shadow of a doubt about it."

For several days and nights following, poor Mama spent most of her time sitting on a hard kitchen chair by Gyula's bedside, changing his plasters and giving him medicine every few hours. What a relief when the doctor finally declared to the exhausted parents that the crisis was over and the small patient would certainly recover.

And recover he did, but he always had a weakness in his lungs after that. Later, when he started to school, he had to spend several days making tedious visits to the hospital, where he sat with Mama on a hard wooden bench in a barnlike waiting room, until his turn came for that mysterious something called an X ray.

When they called his name, Mama accompanied him to a small room and helped him strip off his shirt and undershirt. A nurse positioned him with his chest pressed against an icy-cold metal frame and told him to stand perfectly still and not to breathe until she said, "Right."

The gloomy dark room had all sorts of fixtures around the walls and pulleys and machines with hissing and buzzing noises coming out at times. Gyula's little heart pounded with fear, and if he had not been so often admonished to be a big brave boy, and if he had not had the confidence that Mama was somewhere close by, he might have forgotten all about the injunction not to breathe and instead burst into terrified tears.

By the time Gyula had reached eight, he had experienced many such X rays. To him it had become old business. Sometimes he began to hold his breath even before the nurse told him to, with the result that by the time she said, "Right," his face was as red as a chicken's comb and his lungs felt almost ready to burst. By this time Gyula had accepted his endless coughs, colds, and wheezing as a legacy for life.

One day while visiting the doctor, the man looked thoughtfully at Gyula. "I wonder whether a change of climate would help?" he mused. "Perhaps a year at Farkasgyepu, the forest school, would make all the difference. I'll see what I can do."

Eventually it was all settled. Gyula would attend the school in the mountains. There sick children could continue their schooling while they were patients.

At first homesickness almost overcame Gyula, but soon he had adjusted and at Farkasgyepu he completed his third year of primary schooling.

Upon returning home to Harsny his cough worsened, and he began to wheeze at an alarming rate. Aunt Bozsike, one of Mama's sisters, who was visiting the family when Gyula returned home, suggested that she take the boy with her to Budapest. "He needs good food to build him up. See how well he did at Farkasgyepu. Yes, Yes," she added, "I know you and his father cannot afford it. Do let him come with me. Imirc and I will care for him as if he were our own son."

So at ten years of age Gyula sampled life in the big city. Aunt Bozsike sent him to school, and he completed his fourth class while there. She also took him to church with her.

Church was not entirely a new experience for the boy. He had sometimes attended special-occasion masses in the village church. He had seen the gold threads glinting in the richly embroidered altar cloths and had smelled the burning candles and dipped his finger in the brass bowl of holy water. But Papa and Mama were not particularly religious. In fact, Aunt Bozsike branded as blasphemous the remarks that Papa muttered about the portly priest who regularly visited the poverty-stricken cobbler's shop and demanded tithes on Papa's small earnings.

But Aunt Bozsike was religious to a fault. She attended church twice each day, and Gyula believed that if the priest had told her to attend four times daily she would have done it. (Later on in her life the priest persuaded her to sell her house and all her possessions and give the money to the church. When Uncle Imirc, a Protestant, objected, she divorced him and fanatically devoted herself to her religion.)

Except for the regular church going and the deluges of religion which washed heedlessly over his head, Gyula enjoyed his year in Budapest. Aunt Bozsike fed him like a king, she bought him new clothes and shoes, she even took an interest in his schooling and personally supervised his homework each night. In all probability she would have kept him in Budapest and cared for him as a son if he had paid more attention to her efforts with catechism and rosary beads.

As it was, when the school year ended Aunt Bozsike pronounced him cured and took him back home to Harsny.

Now Gyula was old enough to help earn his keep, and after school and on weekends he joined his older brothers in working at the local bowling alley. During school holidays the three found employment in a soda-water factory. It was Gyula's job to wash and rinse the bottles; Istvan and Andras filled and capped them. The filling machine fascinated Gyula. He never tired of watching as Istvan pushed each freshly rinsed bottle under the spout, leaned hard on the pump handle, and the soda water hissed and bubbled into the bottle. Gyula marveled that the pump always dispensed exactly the right amount—never so much that it overflowed, and never too little to fill the bottle. He longed for the day when he would be promoted to operating that wonderful machine.

When paydays came around there was no boyish planning and wondering what to do with the money they had earned. They took it home to Mama, every forint of it, and her magic touch seemed to make it stretch like elastic. When there was no work available in the soda-water factory the older boys hired out as farm helpers, ploughing, hoeing weeds, doing any job that came their way.

As Gyula grew out of his fine city clothes, they passed down to Laszlo. Gyula had to wear hand-me-downs that had already served his two older brothers. No wonder that he shivered in the harsh Hungarian winters and suffered one cold after another. One year he and Andras had to drop out of school because they had no boots to wear.

Perhaps Gyula might have managed a wry smile if he had heard the old saying, "The cobbler's children wear no boots." It was so true in their house.

Sometime in 1940 news of the war in Europe seeped into the Nagy home, but it did not affect them then nearly as much as the suggestion that Mama made on that very same day.

"Papa," she said looking across to where Papa sat gulping coffee from an enamel mug, his sleeves rolled up and his elbows planted firmly on the end of the supper table. "Why don't we sell this house and move to Budapest? I've heard that there are better opportunities for work in the city."

Papa almost dropped his mug of hot coffee. His mouth fell open and he looked as if he were going to say something, but no sound came. Watching him, Mama added hastily, "You could keep on with your shoemaking, of course, but maybe the boys and I could rent a stall at one of the markets. I've been told there's a good living for anyone who's willing to work."

Mama's words stirred the family like a wasp in a beehive. After the initial shock everyone began talking at once. Each one had a different suggestion or observation to make. Voices rose in a buzzing crescendo as each one struggled to be heard.

Finally Papa held up his hand for silence. "We shall have to discuss the matter from all angles," he said with a dignity befitting the head of the household. "This is no small step to take. Nagys and Kisses (Mama's family) have lived in this village for generations—"

"But they don't have to die here," sixteen-year-old Istvan interrupted impudently.

His father silenced him with a frown and continued, "But if we can better ourselves by uprooting, then—"

It did not take long to dispose of the old house and move their meager belongings to a city apartment on the outskirts of Pest.

As they watched the Nagys go, the neighbors shook their heads and predicted all kinds of dire disasters. But Mama set her lips in determined fashion and said that it would be difficult to be in worse circumstances than they already were, and anyway one could only wait and see.

Not that Mama did any waiting. The last pot and pan had scarcely been stacked in the new kitchen's cupboards before she and Istvan were off to the markets to make arrangements.

From then on, as Gyula remembers, it was nothing but work, work, and more work. Schooldays, except for Laszlo and Mariska, were gone forever. While Papa worked at home in the cozy kitchen making thigh boots and cobbling shoes, Mama and Istvan and Andras shivered their way to the railway station to meet the early-morning trains that brought fresh fruit and vegetables to the city.

Gyula went with them often enough to know the routine. While they waited in the huge marketplace, agents collected the crates and baskets of produce and auctioned them off to the highest bidder. Mama soon learned how to purchase her daily requirements of cabbages and beets and bright orange carrots; red peppers and turnips; rosy apples and purple grapes. The look of them was enough to make one hungry, but the boys rarely sampled the produce; they knew all too well that every grape or apple eaten devoured the small profits that Mama made.

Instead they loaded the goods onto the heavy steel-framed wooden trolley that was strong enough to carry a half ton and concentrated on pushing and pulling it through the cobbled streets to the suburban market where Mama had her stall.

In dawn's gray light dozens of such laden carts lumbered through the city streets on their way to smaller markets. Sometimes a cabbage or an onion fell off and lay unheeded in the mud or, catastrophe of catastrophes, a top-heavy trolley overbalanced and scattered its load. Then any other vendors within sight and hearing left their loads and hurried back to help. Who knew when they might suffer a similar misfortune?

Because of Gyula's weak lungs, Mama considered the market work too heavy for him, and presently he found a job as a delivery boy for a local grocer. The work was not too arduous and the hours were nowhere near as long as at the markets. In fact, Gyula concluded that riding his employer's bicycle around all day and delivering groceries could almost be considered a congenial pastime.

What matter that at fourteen his formal schooling had finished in class six? Gyula had no dreams. No plans for the future. Poverty had been his companion for most of his life. What else was there but to strive to fill one's stomach and clothe one's body? To accomplish this one had to work; there was no other honest way. The poor rarely had time to indulge in ambitious dreams.

When Istvan found a better-paying job, Gyula had to take his place helping his mother at the markets. He was older now and grown into a husky teenager, and Mama hoped that he could stand the early hours in the cold and in the damp or rainy weather.

But after a very few months his cough worsened, and he wheezed as he pushed the heavy trolley back and forth.

Now Mama had another of her brilliant ideas. She consulted with one of her wealthy sisters whose eldest daughter held a responsible secretarial position in the Ford Motor Company in Budapest. Surely, said Mama, a girl in that position would know what apprenticeships were offered. Perhaps she could pull a string here and there, and be compassionate to a delicate but hard-working relative.

Blood being thicker than water, as the saying goes, the niece did her best, and in October 1943, when he was seventeen years old, Gyula Nagy became an apprenticed motor mechanic. The small wage he earned scarcely covered his tram fares.

"But that doesn't matter," Mama declared. "Gyula is too delicate for heavy work. This way he will learn a fine trade, yes? Two years is not long to wait."

By this time war's deadly tentacles had reached across Europe and caught nonbelligerent Hungary in their grasp. Six months after Gyula commenced work at the Ford Motor Company, German troops entered Hungary and rounded up nearly half a million Jews and dissidents and deported them to the concentration camps and gas ovens. Then the Americans, in their efforts to dislodge the Germans, began to bomb Budapest.

The Nagys lived in a small housing commission apartment close to an important industrial area, so they never knew what hour of the day or night the planes would zoom across the city and drop their deadly loads.

At fifty-one Papa was too old to go to war. Instead he gave up his unprofitable shoemaking and helped Mama with her fruit and vegetable stall. Istvan and Andras were drafted into the army and marched off to Germany. Of course, Mama cried as she watched them go.

War wasn't noble and heroic, she said. It was a wicked breaking of women's hearts and wasting of young men's lives. Both she and

Papa remembered World War I and the terrible things that happened in France and Germany and Belgium then.

It was no use for her to hope that when Gyula's turn came he would be declared medically unfit and escape the draft. In Hungary in those days there was no time for anything like a physical examination or army training. Young men were called up, handed a gun and a box of cartridges, and sent off to shoot the enemy.

"It's wicked, simply wicked," Mama said as she wept. But nobody listened to her, least of all the War Office.

Gyula greeted his eighteenth birthday with a mixture of trepidation and excitement. He knew there was no chance of his escaping the draft. Every young man had to serve his country whether he was motivated by patriotism or not. Day by day he anxiously awaited the dreaded summons.

In November Gyula was called up into the labor corps and sent to work digging tank traps in a desperate Hungarian effort to stop the Russian army from marching into Budapest. He had mixed feelings about this assignment. Certainly there was nothing noble or exciting about toiling from dawn till dusk throwing spadefuls of earth out of a deepening hole. He wasn't likely to lose his life digging tank traps, not unless the earth sides caved in and buried him or the American Air Force came over and bombed the city—and they did that every day anyhow.

A month later Gyula was back at his old job. Ford Motor Company's factory had been requisitioned for essential war production, and they needed all the workers that they had trained.

As the weeks passed, Hungary's position grew more and more desperate. German troops overran the west part of Hungary, and Russia hammered on its eastern frontiers. Placards appeared on the streets insisting that all males aged between 16 and 48 must report to the army. Hungarian girls refused to speak to any man in that age group who was not actively defending his country.

"There's nothing else for us to do," Gyula told Laszlo one early morning as they trundled Mama's heavy trolley to the market. With Papa and Mama getting on in years and the older brothers off to war, the two youths often helped out at the markets before beginning their own day's work.

"What do you mean?" Laszlo puffed. His breath hung in a white cloud in front of his face.

"I've heard that if they don't get enough volunteers, they'll make a house-to-house search." Gyula shrugged. "You're not safe anywhere, not even at Ford."

"We'd be worse off if they caught us." Laszlo grimaced. "I guess we'd better go along."

When they told Mama their decision she threw her apron over her head and sobbed quietly into its voluminous folds. But they had no option.

"Take some food with you," she urged them before they set off next morning. "Papa's friends say that the army is very disorganized. There are not enough uniforms and no blankets; only the officers are properly fed." Tears spilled down her thin cheeks as she hacked off great chunks of bread while her sons wrapped them in newspaper and stuffed them into their pockets.

"Don't worry, Mama." Gyula kissed her on both cheeks, bade Papa good-bye, and set off with Laszlo for the recruiting office.

Long before they reached the given address they saw the crowd of men and boys milling around the entrance and overflowing onto the pavement outside the drab government building. Many of them had gravitated into small groups and were talking and joking and laughing rather too uproariously to be natural, Gyula thought. Some registered no emotion at all, just stamped their cold feet and blew on their fingers as if powered by clockwork. Others stood silent and sullen, nervously puffing on ersatz cigarettes. Gyula and Laszlo found places among the stragglers waiting at the foot of the steps.

A freezing cold wind funneled along the street, leaving snowflakes in its wake. The shivering men pushed and elbowed their way into the shelter of the building. Hours dragged by and the crowd seemed no less. As fast as those at the front of the line disappeared behind the heavy doors, other conscripts swelled the numbers at the back.

At last it was the Nagys' turn. A harrassed official shoved a pile of papers across his desk and told the brothers to fill them in. "Some in duplicate, some triplicate; the directions are on them. When you've finished take them to that man over by the window. Next?"

Filling in those inquisitive forms seemed to Gyula to be only a shade less strenuous than digging tank traps. But at last they were finished, and he and Laszlo presented themselves to the man by the window.

"All right, men," the officer sitting at a battered table took their sheafs of papers and stuffed them into an already bulging file. "There's a war on and the sooner you get into it the better." He waved toward a motley collection of trucks and buses parked at the back of the building. "They're waiting to take you to the railway station. You'll be off to Germany tonight."

More hours passed as the waiting vehicles slowly filled with men of all ages, shapes, and sizes. Dusk had drawn its gray curtain across the city by the time they rattled into the station, where impatient officers hustled them along the platform and into unlit, unheated train compartments.

More waiting, and then when they had given up hope of anything happening, there was a sudden jerk and they were off. A hushed cheer went up from the men in Gyula's carriage as the train crawled slowly through the city suburbs. The ones near the windows squinted into the darkness, trying to identify silhouetted landmarks.

"There's the river. That's the Elizabeth Bridge." "No, it's the—" "We're going west, see there's the—"

A dozen men in each compartment were lucky enough to get seats. The rest lounged in the corridors or squatted uncomfortably on the floor, huddling together for warmth. The brothers squeezed into the small space on the floor between the seats, their backs to the side wall. Few slept.

For most of the night the train snailed along, steaming and jerking and grinding, stopping and starting. Rumors throbbed back and forth between the carriages: "The tracks have been blown up.

There's a derailed train ahead. The bridge is out. The war's over!''

Only a few guessed what later proved to be the truth, that the Russians had completely surrounded Budapest and that the train could not find a way out.

Finally, in the early hours of the morning the train ground to a halt, and word passed along that the men were to alight. Wearily they tumbled onto the platform of a small station.

"Esztergom Tabor," one of the men shouted his recognition. "That's almost next door to the city. All those hours in the train and we've only come 60 kilometers.''

A couple of weary-looking officers appeared out of the darkness and ordered the bedraggled company to follow them to a nearby army camp for the rest of the night.

Next morning Gyula forced his bleary eyes open to a scene of indescribable disorder. From every room, hallway and office, disheveled men and boys wandered about like lost sheep. No one knew where to go or what to do. The few officers of the night before seemed to have vanished. There was no sign of cookhouse or store. Except for the overnight influx of raw recruits the barracks was empty.

"This is no good." One of the men standing near to the brothers blew on his cold fingers and stamped his feet. "I'm cold and I'm hungry and can't see any sense in standing around here waiting for something to happen. Let's go."

He strode in the direction of the unguarded gates, and after a moment's hesitation the brothers followed him.

"Where'll we go?" Laszlo asked as they caught up with the man.

"Well, I'm going back home to Pest." The man squared his shoulders defiantly. "If they want me they can come and get me. I did my part. I answered the call-up."

Gyula nodded his agreement. "We'd better not go along the main road though; there seem to be all kinds of army trucks racing back and forth."

"We can follow a back route across the mountains. I know this district like the back of my hand."

All day the three tramped along winding trails and climbed steep wooded hills. Several times they paused to drink at ice-cold streams and munch the hard bread that Mama had provided. Gyula's feet were blistered, and he longed to rest awhile. But the man urged them on. "We must get to the railway. We'd freeze if we had to spend a night in the open."

At ten o'clock at night the exhausted trio staggered into Szentendre, the terminus of the city train line, and found the small station swarming with men who had taken a shorter route than they. The last night train had already left for Budapest, but with nearly two hundred cold and hungry men angrily demanding transport, the station master soon found a way of getting an extra train to take the men to Budapest.

"Oh, it will be so good to get home again." Gyula huddled in a corner of the comfortless coach and pulled his coat tightly about him.

"Don't forget the bridges," their companion yawned. "The train stops at the Danube. That's great for the ones living on the right bank, but you have to get over to the left, same as me, don't you?"

"What's wrong with the bridges?" Laszlo spoke up.

"Nothing, except that the German army controls Budapest, remember. Every bridge will be guarded as if it were a jewel. We'll be lucky if we get home tonight."

The man's prediction proved correct. When the throng of would-be soldiers stumbled out of the train at midnight, those who lived on the right side of the Danube melted off into the darkness. The rest traipsed through the deserted streets and tried the Margaret Bridge.

No. The Germans on guard duty threatened to open fire if they did not make themselves scarce.

"Let's try the Chain Bridge."

Again the armed guards angrily waved them away, and no amount of arguing could change their minds.

"Let's go to the Elizabeth. I'm going to try every bridge that spans the river," one of the men said.

The guards at the Elizabeth Bridge lowered their rifles and listened as Toni, the leader, tried a different tack. Raising his arms above his head in a reassuring gesture, he stepped forward and explained their predicament.

Perhaps it was Toni their leader's eloquence, or perhaps it was the sight of nearly one hundred shivering, woebegone men grouped behind him that moved the guard to take a risk.

"All right," said the officer in charge. "Line up here. I'll send a soldier to take you across. He'll march behind you. One bit of funny business and he fires. Understand?"

"Yes, sir," Toni said and the weary recruits murmured their assent.

When Gyula tapped on the back door of their home, and Papa finally heard and let them in, Mama cried again. But this time they were tears of joy.

"Oh, my poor, poor lads," she crooned and bustled about stirring up the fire and preparing a hot drink to warm their insides.

"Such as it is," she mourned. "We have no coffee, no tea, no milk. Everything is ersatz. The German army has taken all the food. Ah, it is hard even to get bread these days. As for the market! Every day less and less food comes in from the country. And the price of it! Only the rich can buy."

Ersatz or not, the hot drink had the desired effect, and the youthful soldier-civilians thankfully spent the remainder of that eventful night safe and warm in their own beds.

Morning light brought a sobering realization. Gyula and Laszlo would now be classed as army deserters, and if the German or Hungarian Nazis smelled them out they would be shot on sight. The thought of such a fate terrified the family more than the bombing planes that daily sent them scurrying into neighborhood bunkers.

"You'll have to hide," Papa said. Mama nodded vigorously. "You can't go back to work; you'd be caught immediately. The Nazis are everywhere. You can't trust anyone. Even the walls have ears."

Two weeks of hiding was more than enough for Gyula. He couldn't stand the uncertainty and the inactivity.

"I'm going down to reenlist," he told Laszlo. "It's bad to be involved in a war but it's worse to be hiding like—like a rat in a sewer."

"I'll come too." Laszlo snatched up his cap. "Let's take a blanket with us this time."

With Budapest surrounded by Russian troops and the fall of the city imminent, the army recruiting office appeared even more disorganized than before.

"All right, boys," said the officer who took their names and particulars. "Here's a rifle each and a box of cartridges. We have no uniforms, which is probably just as well—you can pass for civilians if the Russians catch you. Go over to that fellow in the corner, and he will show you how to use your rifles."

The man in the corner wasted neither time nor words in his instructions. Twice he showed the brothers how to load and unload their rifles, how to whip the weapon quickly to the shoulder and fire. Then he made them go over the actions half a dozen times before actually sequeezing the trigger of the empty gun. "Squeeze, don't jerk," he said. "Yes, like that—only don't forget to load the bullets in before you face the Reds."

A few more words of advice and then he waved them on. A junior officer near the outer door told them which streets they were to defend.

"Hang around the street corners as often as you can," he said, "but there's an army bunker in the nearby square. You'll be spending most of your time in that." He swore under his breath. "The cursed Reds are not giving us a chance."

For weeks Budapest lay under siege. Bombarded day and night by Russian shells, the terrified inhabitants spent most of their time in the bunkers. The newly inducted soldiers found little to do but crouch in the shelters along with a lot of other new recruits. Shells exploded all around them, and they had no way of hitting back at the unseen enemy.

Days of almost constant firing passed. Food became even more scarce than before. Water mains were put out of action, and men had to sneak out under cover of darkness and try to fetch buckets of drinking water. Sanitation suffered.

And then one dreadful day when shells rained over the city like a deadly hailstorm, Gyula, squatting near the entrance to the bunker, saw one hit only a few yards away.

"Watch out!" he yelled and felt himself flung backward by the force of the blast.

Fear masked his pain, and not until his mates dragged him into sandbagged safety and tried to stanch the flow of blood, did he realize that shell fragments had entered his left shoulder, arm, and leg.

There was no question of getting to a hospital. Anyone venturing outside of the shelter would have been mown down like summer grass.

"I've seen a first-aid kit around here somewhere." Laszlo, whitefaced and trembling, felt around in a box of supplies.

"Give it to me. I'll bandage him up." One of the older men held out his hand for the kit. "I used to be a hospital orderly."

It was rough-and-ready doctoring, but it stopped the bleeding and helped Gyula psychologically. He was young and had no thought of dying. He knew nothing about septic wounds and other terrible possiblities. Sure it was painful, but given a little time the wounds would heal. He was lucky to have escaped so lightly.

Brave thoughts, but the next few days and nights were such nightmares of pain and soreness that Gyula wished with all his might that he were a child again, back in Harsny village under the care of dear old doctor Papp.

Then something happened that made him forget all about the past and the present and filled him with shuddering forebodings for the future. He awoke one morning to hear the man next to him saying, "My gun's gone."

Stiffly he raised himself on his right elbow and felt around for his own rifle. It was gone. A premonition of peril clutched his heart.

"So is mine," he choked.

"So is mine." "And mine." "And mine." Voices all around the bunker echoed the same discovery.

With paling faces the defenders of Budapest stared at one another. They knew what it meant. They'd heard. This was the usual pattern. The traitors in their midst had stolen their guns and surrendered to the enemy.

Before they had time to decide on a course of action a Russian officer appeared at the entrance of their bunker.

"All out," he ordered in strangely accented Hungarian. "Collect your belongings and file out ahead of me."

Sullenly the soldiers obeyed. Once outside the bunker the silence of the deserted streets hit them like a physical blow. There was no mistaking it. The shelling had stopped. The Russians were in charge of the city.

"March." The Russian officer urged them along the streets like animals being driven to the slaughter yards. At every corner other groups of captured Hungarian soldiers swelled the company. Numbly they trudged the snow-sludged streets until they reached an abandoned school on the outskirts of Buda.

There were water taps at the school and little else. No food, no bedding, no bunks. By nightfall the men's stomachs growled with hunger. Next morning they were marched out to the inadequate toilets and then herded onto the road again and walked all day. That night they slept in the open, and Gyula's wounds ached with the cold. The third day they marched farther to a village called Gödöllö, now occupied by the Russians.

"Aren't they ever going to give us something to eat?" Laszlo whispered. Among the hundreds of captured soldiers he had somehow managed to stay close to Gyula.

Gyula shook his head. "Rotten curs. See what they're doing now."

The Russian soldiers billeted in the village were moving in and out among the captives, stripping them of any quality clothing that they wore. Warm wool coats and fleecy lined trousers were exchanged for threadbare Russian uniforms. If a Hungarian objected he was threatened or clubbed with a rifle butt. A big man standing beside Gyula was forced to give up his almost-new thick-soled leather boots. In return the Russian soldier threw him his worn footgear, many sizes too small.

In vain the poor man tried to force his feet into the battered boots. For the rest of the terrible journey he trudged barefooted through the snow.

That night the cold and hungry men were crowded into an empty barracks, but no matter how they pushed and shoved and no matter how loudly their captors yelled and cursed, there wasn't room enough for all. Gyula and Laszlo were among the overflow that had to spend the night in the open.

Utterly exhausted, they threw themselves onto the hard ground and huddled together under the blanket that Laszlo had brought from home. In the morning they awoke to find themselves covered with freshly fallen snow.

"We're lucky we're young enough to survive." Gyula spoke in a low voice as he clasped his hands across his empty stomach. He and Laszlo watched in silent indignation as the Russian soldiers tramped around the compound, booting the men who still lay sleeping under the snow. Despite repeated kickings and cursings some were too weak to rise, and the soldiers angrily booted them aside and left the freezing elements to do their deathly work.

The rest of the struggling captives squeezed into the barracks, and the Russians began to sort their catch. Man after starving man stumbled forward, was questioned by a hard-eyed officer seated at a makeshift desk, and then shunted into one of several groups.

Fear gripped Gyula's heart when his turn came and the officer ordered him to join about a hundred other wounded men on the far side of the room. What would happen to Laszlo? While they remained together Gyula felt that somehow he could protect his younger brother. But now—

The officer pointed Laszlo toward a dozen or so other beardless youths, and Gyula made an impulsive attempt to accompany his brother. A cursing soldier with a gun roughly elbowed them apart. (Years later Gyula learned that the boys had spent two weeks in a camp and then their captors set them free. It was the only kind thing he ever heard about how the Russians treated their prisoners).

Gyula never knew what happened to the unwounded prisoners. As soon as the sorting process ended, a double handful of Russian guards marched the wounded men out of the building, and once more they plodded hopelessly along the slushy road.

"How long do they expect us to survive without food?" The man alongside Gyula muttered the question out of the side of his mouth.

Gyula shook his head. Fistfuls of snow, grabbed in passing, assuaged their thirst and set their already chilled bodies shivering, but food? How long, indeed, could their already thin bodies stand it?

Heads down and shoulders sagging, the wounded men trudged wearily along country roads and through villages where they knew the fearful inhabitants were peering at them from behind drawn curtains.

Five kilometers. Ten kilometers. Would it never end?

All at once Gyula became aware of a surging excitement in the ranks, a rising murmur, a quickening of pace. He lifted his head.

"Look!" the man beside him exclaimed and lurched toward the side of the road.

For a split second Gyula stood bewildered; then he joined the mad scramble of men breaking ranks and dashing into a nearby cabbage patch.

The cabbages had long since been cut and carted away but the withered stalks and roots still dotted the muddy field.

The shouting guards rushed about, cursing and clubbing the men back onto the road but not before each captive had grabbed at least one stalk.

There wasn't much nourishment in a cabbage stalk, but Gyula blissfully sucked and chewed on his prize. That, and a handful of grain snatched from a passing cart, kept him going for another two days.

Eventually the sorry group halted in front of a building where in better days, cartloads of beets had been processed into sugar. Now the huge abandoned plant served as a military hospital.

"No room. There's no room here." The words passed down the line and dispelled any hopes the captives had that their journey's end was in sight. Russians at the hospital ordered them to line up for a ration of black bread and a mug of ersatz coffee and then they waved them on again.

Two more days of nightmarish trudging brought the bedraggled company to a deserted high school at Jaszbereny.

Was this it? Would they stop here? Gyula's exhausted body had long since lost all sense of particular pain. His untended wounds and swollen, blistered feet; his frost-bitten face and hands; his starving stomach; all blended into one huge agony.

He almost collapsed with relief when their captors herded them inside the building. In each room wide wooden shelves doubled as makeshift beds, enough for all.

Shelter at last. Gyula sank onto the nearest bunk. Now, if only they would give him food.

Prisoner of War

Early the next morning, the wounded who could still walk lined up for a breakfast of black bread and watery coffee. Then the guards ordered them into a large room to wait for medical attention. The room smelled of carbolic acid, but there its resemblance to a hospital ended. There were no freshly painted white walls; no glass-fronted cupboards full of gleaming instruments; no sound of hissing steam sterilizers.

Soon Gyula's turn came for medical attention. A grim-faced orderly pushed him into a room with barred windows and an armed guard. A Russian doctor questioned him, and then with an expression of extreme distaste subjected him to a hasty physical examination, changed the filthy, blood stiffened bandages, and handed him a couple pills to swallow. Another guard shunted him through a side door and told him to return to the barracks. That was the sum total of Gyula's medical care. But after a week of weary trudging and near starvation he felt grateful for any semblance of shelter and a daily ration of food—no matter how meager.

Six days passed by before Gyula was declared fit and told he would be sent to a prisoner-of-war camp. He joined the shivering rows of men lined up outside the makeshift hospital. Russian guards cursed the ragged ranks into some semblance of order and marched them through the village to their new location a few kilometers away.

The main buildings of the huge prisoner-of-war camp had window holes with no frames or glass windowpanes. Doorways with no doors. Steep staircases with no handrails. Rumor had it that the buildings had been a Hungarian army barracks in the process of being remodeled when war came. Because of lack of funds and material the army had relinquished the project. Now the Russians had taken over and billeted their prisoners there.

The new prisoners soon settled into the routine of the huge camp full of German and Hungarian soldiers. Apart from meal-time, when they all lined up for their scanty rations, and all-too-short exercise period, there was nothing to do. Except for the few fortunates detailed to help the cooks, the rest of the prisoners spent their days in idleness.

"I thought the Russians slaved their prisoners to death." Gyula said to one of the men who had been there long before Gyula arrived.

The man shrugged. "I think it's because they don't have enough men to guard us. There's work to do, but they're afraid we might escape if we were allowed outside."

So the men lounged around or crowded into each other's barracks and talked and swapped past experiences. A few tried singing patriotic songs, but the guards soon stopped that.

Now that he felt better, the inactivity grated on Gyula's nerves, and he was glad one morning when a guard chose him and another youth named Janos, for a work assignment.

"Go downstairs and help the doctor," he ordered.

Mystified, they carefully negotiated the perilous stairs and made their way to what had once been the spacious foyer of the army building.

"Wonder what we'll have to do?" The youth at Gyula's side mouthed the words. Gyula shook his head. He had no clue.

They entered the doorway and Gyula, in the lead, stopped short. The foyer's floor was strewn with frozen, naked corpses—dead men already robbed of clothes and dignity.

"Hurry up!" A sharp voice pierced through Gyula's horror. A Russian woman doctor waited for them beside a large table. Without further waste of words she indicated that they were to lift the corpses one by one onto the table and remove them as she finished.

Gyula's horrified mind rebelled, but his terrified body obeyed. With Janos taking the head and he the feet, they lifted the first stiff body up onto the table and stood back to watch.

The woman picked up a tiny knife and bent over the body. With one quick movement she slashed a line down the abdomen and then proceeded to follow it with a deeper cut. It must have been hard work because Gyula noticed that she grunted and sweated as the task progressed.

Once the incision was complete she poked and peered inside the body.

Gyula gasped and shut his eyes. What was she looking for? His head reeled. He recalled tales of escapees, wealthy Jews, who swallowed their jewelry and gold in an effort to get it out of the country. But these men weren't Jews. Or were they? Who could tell.

The doctor straightened up. "Next," she called and Janos and Gyula advanced to lift that body down and replace it with another.

Body after body. Cut after slash, cut after slash, cut—

Gyula gulped to control his stomach's heavings and tried to concentrate on the doctor's hands. She didn't appear to be finding any valuables. He shuddered. Maybe she was a student. Maybe she was—what did they call it—performing autopsies—trying to find out why the men had died.

He could tell her. Men died every night. Some who tried to find their way downstairs to the latrine fell over the side of the unrailed staircase. They pitched headlong onto the concrete floor two or three stories below. Older men died of dysentery, exhaustion, untreated illnesses.

There were other causes. The camp latrine consisted of a five-meter-deep pit about seven meters long and three meters wide, with narrow timbers laid at regular intervals across it. There was no covering, no privacy. In cold and rain the sodden timbers became as slick as ice. Men weakened by dysentery sometimes lost their footing. There was no way of rescuing them from their ghastly grave.

Despite himself Gyula gagged at the recollection of what he'd seen, and the doctor glanced at him impatiently. She said nothing.

At last the dreadful task ended, and the youths left the foyer in time to join the mealtime queue. Gyula tried to shut out the memory of this terrible experience by thinking about food. Food usually dominated his thoughts by day and haunted his dreams at night. That, and how to escape from the Russians were the only subjects that interested the semi-starving men in the camp. Sure they were given enough bread and watery soup to keep them alive, but just barely.

Some of the German prisoners haunted the garbage pile at the back of the camp kitchen and foraged through the refuse for anything edible. With guttural exclamations of satisfaction they seized the used soup bones and gnawed off the remaining shreds of tasteless meat or cracked the bones and sucked out the marrow.

Some of the other men became past masters at the art of scrounging. Paper and pencils mysteriously disappeared from Russian offices and just as mysteriously reappeared in the prisoners' barracks. Eager hands tore the paper into smaller pieces and handed it around. The men wrote notes to their loved ones and as opportunity offered wrapped the missives around pebbles and tossed them over the wall—hoping that they would be picked up by kind-hearted civilians who would see to it that they reached their destination.

"It's the end of March today," one of the men, who had managed to keep track of time, made the announcement to the miserable assembly.

End of March. Gyula counted back. He and Laszlo had reenlisted early in January. Nearly two months he had been in this prisoner-of-war camp. Would he stay here until war's end?

His question received an answer a few days later when word passed around that the prisoners were going to be moved. But where? Where to? Muttered speculations spread throughout the camp and accelerated when officials announced that they would be moved by train.

Terror gripped Gyula's heart. Wheels instead of walking meant only one thing. They were being sent to Russia. All he'd ever heard of Siberian slave camps sprang into his mind—cruelty beyond belief, eternally frozen terrain that prevented escape, slow, torturous death. This was the fate he'd dreaded from the first day of his capture.

"Romania. We're going to Romania." One of the prisoners understood a little Russian, and he passed the overheard word around.

Guards marched the apprehensive men to a siding and herded them forty at a time into filthy cattle cars. When the full quota was aboard, a guard slammed the door and bolted and locked it on the outside. The only light and air entered through cracks in the wooden walls.

Day after day the men stood jammed together like sardines in a tin. The train jolted and swayed its way across Romania, and the prisoners cursed in helpless, hopeless anger. They had no food and only two buckets of water and a single dipper between forty thirsty men. Another battered bucket passed around served their creature needs.

Once a day when the train stopped at a station for an unusually long time, the guards unlocked the doors and allowed one prisoner out to empty the latrine and refill the water buckets.

At one busy station the waterman carried the buckets out from Gyula's wagon and did not return. Hour after hour the thirsty men waited until at last they realized that the water carrier had escaped. Tormented by thirst the other thirty-nine growled under their breath, but no one complained aloud. In their hearts they all envied him his luck.

Not until late at night when the guards made a hasty, last minute head count before the train pulled out, was the escape discovered. Cursing and shouting at the tops of their voices the guards grabbed the Romanian on duty in the station's signal office. Ignoring the bewildered man's sobbing protests they bundled him into the cattle car and locked the door. A minute later and the engine hissed and ground on its way.

The men talked as the train rattled over the tracks. No one could overhear them now. They sorted themselves out into more congenial groups, German with German, Hungarian with Hungarian. The boundaries narrowed further as the men swapped names and cities and places of work.

"I worked at the Ford Motor Company in Budapest." It was Gyula's turn to introduce himself.

"Did you?" A delighted voice spoke out of the gloom. "So did I. Let's stick together, buddy."

A man named Tamas wormed his way through the pack of men until he stood near Gyula. He was several years older and had finished his apprenticeship a year before Gyula began.

"I wonder whether we'll ever get out of this alive and go back to the old factory," Tamas mused aloud.

Gyula answered with a grunt.

For ten days or more the men huddled in the cattle cars while the train snorted idly at deserted sidings more often than it moved. The men jammed nearest to the walls put their eyes to the cracks and reported what little they saw of outside goings on.

Once a day the guards came around with a ration of bread and water, but not even the water was sufficient. When the train finally halted and the bolts were drawn back the released men tumbled out and ran to bury their faces in the puddles of melted snow alongside the tracks.

"*Davaj! Davaj!*" The waiting guards shouted and furiously charged in and out among the crouching men. "Into the trucks. Go!" The guards pushed and prodded the men toward waiting trucks.

Eventually the pandemonium died down as truckload after truckload of weary, despairing men rumbled off into the darkness. Gyula and Tamas clung together, trying to keep their balance as the driver sped dangerously over narrow, unpaved roads.

"Last day of April 1945," Tamas muttered close to Gyula's ear, "first day of—who knows what?"

Darkness prevented the new arrivals from seeing much of their new prison that night, but bright searchlights on towers around the perimeter told Gyula that they must be well inside Russian-controlled territory, far enough from the war zone to be secure from enemy air attack.

Morning strengthened his conviction. After a breakfast of the usual black bread and warm, watery soup, the men lined up for registration. A hulking officer with cold gray eyes recorded their names, ages, addresses, and occupations; then, with a jerk of his massive head, directed them into another room to await instructions and work assignment.

Any tradesmen among the nearly 2000 prisoners found work in the prison's tailor shop, or cobbled, or cooked, or cut hair. Because they were experienced mechanics Gyula and Tamas and five other men went to work in the garage outside the prison camp. The camp commander owned a car, and a dilapidated fleet of trucks served to transport people and supplies.

The rest of the prisoners worked at dismantling the ruined parts of the old sugar factory that served as barracks; cleaning bricks, cutting iron girders, straightening crooked nails knocked out of old timbers.

Only a three-strand barbed-wire fence around the camp prevented the prisoners' escape, and the guards themselves exhibited a laxity that amazed Gyula.

"They never send a guard out with us," he remarked to Tamas as the seven mechanics showed their passes at the gate and then passed through on their way to the workshop.

"They don't need to," Tamas shrugged. "They know that we can't escape. The Russians themselves are not allowed to move more than forty kilometers without a special permit." He spat contemptuously and wiped his mouth with his sleeve. "We're surrounded by Russian villagers who wouldn't dare to help us. I've heard that several have tried to escape—they didn't get far."

The hopelessness of it depressed Gyula, but not for long. At eighteen and a half one cannot remain despairing. Besides, he could have been so much worse off. At least there was no outright cruelty here. No sadistic tortures such as he'd heard of happening in other camps. Sure, the guards counted heads each morning and on the rare occasion that someone was missing, security tightened and the guards sneered at the foolish futility of trying to escape. But there were no terrible reprisals on the other men. Indeed, Gyula told himself, he could be grateful that he was here and not slaving in a Siberian mine.

Weeks lengthened into months. Summer came and went. A dry summer. Peasants from the surrounding villages complained uselessly of drought. Cabbages, their main source of food and income, grew no hearts, only bitter outside leaves.

In autumn the prison yard filled with cabbages faster than the men assigned to the task could chop them into sauerkraut. Then came an out-of-season snowfall and the cabbages froze in the mud.

"Where do they store it all?" Gyula asked as he returned from work and saw the cabbage choppers still bending to their task.

"They have concrete tanks under the kitchen, colossal vats. The men throw sackfuls of salt and then tramp up and down, mixing it in with their feet. It's as dark as hades down there." Gyula's informant laughed shortly. "Yesterday one of the fellows dropped his hurricane lamp into the cabbage—we'll have kerosene flavored sauerkraut. You see if we don't."

They did. On the rare occasions that sauerkraut featured in the prisoners' scanty fare, one mouthful tasted of kerosene and the next mouthful tasted as bitter as gall.

"We've got a different job for you two," the garage manager said one day to Tamas and Gyula. "Take those spades. The driver will show you what to do."

They knew better than to ask questions. They picked up the spades and climbed onto the back of the rickety truck that the manager indicated. The driver revved the ancient motor and backed out to the road.

Snow blanched the dreary landscape, and silhouetted trees raised skeleton branches skyward as if imploring mercy from the elements. A biting wind made sport of Gyula's thin coat, but he scarcely noticed its chill. His heart pounded with the joy of being so far outside of those confining barracks.

The truck rattled through a nearby village and Gyula nodded to himself. He knew this place well. Once a week, if they were lucky, armed guards marched prisoners to the village bathhouse.

On again, through another compact village, and another. Suddenly the driver slammed on the brakes and swerved off the road, nearly pitching Tamas and Gyula headlong from the back of the truck.

"There." He pointed to what looked like a cemetery.

Tamas and Gyula picked up their spades and followed him across the snow.

Gyula's spade clanked as if it had struck iron. Again and again he tried to thrust it into the frigid earth. Hack, chip, hack. Fragment by fragment the frozen soil gave way. Hack, hack, chip.

The guard squatted on an overturned tombstone and slapped his cold hands together as he watched them work. Presently a village boy joined him, and from the fragments of their conversation that Gyula understood he pieced together the story.

It was a grave for Nina that they were digging. Nina, the black-haired girl who drove one of the village trucks back and forth to the camp. Yesterday at dusk she was returning home in the back of another truck when an iron bar protruding from a passing hay cart hit her on the temple.

"Too bad," the guard said feelingly, and then in almost the same breath he yelled at Tamas and Gyula, "Hurry, hurry. We must get back."

Hack, chip, chip, hack. Haste was impossible. Gyula's blistered hands cramped on the spade handle. He gasped and sweated from exertion.

"Hurry." The guard squinted at the westering sun and came to inspect the rough-hewn grave. "It will do," he said and sent the loitering youngster to call the villagers.

The boy ran off and a short time latter a sad procession approached the cemetery. A bearded old man in peasant garments led the way. He carried a small handbag and chanted under his breath. Immediately Gyula's thoughts skipped back to Aunt Bozsike and her religion. This fellow that led the way was the local priest in charge of the funeral proceedings. He felt sure of it.

Behind the priest a half dozen men juggled their silent burden over the rough ground, and the group of women accompanying them sniveled and wiped their eyes with the corners of their aprons.

Quietly the sad little group assembled around the grave and the man in front hurriedly opened his bag. Nervously glancing right and left he took out his vestments and hurriedly drew them over his head.

Then with as much haste as he could decently display he rattled through the burial service. The people chanted their prayers and responses and the service was over. The priest quickly disrobed and with an audible sigh of relief he stuffed the vestments back into his bag:

Aha, thought Gyula, that is just what Aunt Bozsike told me. The Communists have suppressed all religion in Russia. These people must have taken fearful risks to bury their relative with Christian rites. He shrugged. That was their business; religion meant nothing to him. Who would equate a God of love with this dreadful war?

Another summer came and went. Seven days a week the men worked from sunup until sundown. No one thought of playing sick or shirking. A man found in the barracks during daylight hours paid for it with hard labor.

At night after their meager supper the men sat around their rooms and smoked their daily ration of newspaper-wrapped *tabuk*. Some tried to mend their threadbare clothes. Mostly they just talked. Talked about what they would do and where they would go when they were freed. Talked about what they would eat when they got home.

Gyula and the other men thought of little else than food and eating. How could they, when gnawing hunger pains and cramped stomachs constantly reminded them of their need.

"When I get home," Tamas spoke to the dozens of listless men around him, "I'm going to hunt around and find me the youngest, plumpest chicken on the farm and I'll get my wife to roast it with potatoes and onions and I'm going to eat the whole lot myself—all of it.''

"Ja. Chicken! If you could only taste the chicken stew that my wife makes.'' One of the men smacked his chapped lips in ravenous anticipation.

"Nothing could taste better than my mother's apple strudel. We had a stunted apple tree in our backyard, scabby and bent and old as the alps, but you should see the apples it produced. Every year we kids helped with the preserving—''

"We preserved apples too. Jars and jars of them.''

"Borsch. My grandmother came from up north, Kisvarda. She can make borsch as well as any—''

"Goulash for me. I vow I'll eat a bathtubful of it.''

Each man, according to his background, had different longings, but on one thing they all agreed. If they lived to reach home again they would never, never despise any kind of nourishing food that was set before them.

"Not only that,'' Tamas declared passionately, "I intend to have good food no matter what else I might have to go without.''

"The best food.'' Gyula nodded in heartfelt agreement. He folded his arms and pressed them tightly over his empty stomach while he tried to direct his mind into other channels. The weather perhaps—

Would it be another freezing winter? How many of these prisoners around him would actually live to go home again?

Home! Food!

Home. Gyula tried to fix a button on the worn army uniform that had been issued when his own clothes fell to pieces. Home. Food to eat. Good food and plenty of it. Mama's goulash. Mama's soup—so thick the spoon nearly stood up in it. Not warm greasy water with a shred of cabbage floating on the top.

Home. The Red Cross arranged for them to write home once every three months, but in two years he had received only one reply from Mama.

It did not say much. Papa, Laszlo, and Mariska were well. So was she, except for the rheumatism in her knees. Laszlo and Istvan were home again, and they hoped that Andras would be home soon.

That puzzled Gyula. How could they be home? Was the war over?

The crude calendar the men marked on the wall said this was January 1947. For a year past the villagers had taunted as they passed the garage, "Cheer up, soldier, you'll be going home soon."

Even some of the guards winked knowingly and cackled, "*Skoro domji*. The war's over. You can go soon."

The camp generator provided electricity, but as far as Gyula knew no guards or villagers owned a radio. No outside news filtered through the language barrier. Rumors, yes. Rumors eternally racing back and forth. They afforded a few moments' entertainment, even hope, but no one actually believed them.

The war over. Could that be possible when in the camp men still came and went. Many died of malnutrition, dysentery, dropsy— their legs swollen and kidneys failing. There was no hospital or medical care.

Other men came to take their places. Only a few weeks before a whole trainload of young men arrived—captured, they said, in the streets of Budapest. No, of course the war could not be over—not when things like that still happened.

The months crawled slowly by. Work and hunger and sleep; hunger and sleep and work. Winter snows melted and warmth crept back into the sun. Sleep and hunger and work. Life was an inescapable treadmill; work and sleep and hunger and hunger and hunger—

Then, without warning, Gyula awoke one morning to feel a strange tension in the air. A dozen men in his room paced restlessly back and forth like caged animals when their keeper is due.

"It must be true," one of them insisted loudly. "Janos understands some Russian, and he overheard the guards—"

"I don't believe it." The man he spoke to rubbed his bristly chin and shook his head vigorously. "Rumors, just rumors."

"They do it to torment us." A third man scratched his thin chest with clawlike hands. "They—"

What were the men talking about? Gyula lay back and closed his eyes. Were these fellows prowling up and down discussing food or release? It must be one or the other. No one talked about anything else, not for any length of time. But what was the use?

"Out! All out!" Beyond the snatches of nearby conversation Gyula thought he heard distant commands. He screwed his eyelids closed in intense concentration. Yes, there it came again—a little closer. "All out!"

Suddenly a guard poked his head around their doorway and yelled, "Out! All out!"

A moment's stunned silence and then the prisoners crowded to the door. Gyula leaped to his feet and followed them. Were enemy planes approaching? Perhaps the barracks was afire? His numbed mind doused the tiny hope that flickered within. He would not let himself be disappointed.

The men lined up outside the kitchen for their usual ration of bread and watery soup, but they could not help seeing the flotilla of battered buses and trucks drawn up alongside the wire fence. Excitement exploded like a lighted fuse. There was no doubt now that they would be moving, but where to? Would it be for better or for worse?

As fast as they swallowed their hunks of black bread, the guards hustled them into the waiting vehicles. Drivers cursed the ancient motors into life, and they roared off down the road—first stop 40 kilometers away.

"There're scarcely any guards around," Tamas muttered to Gyula as the men spilled out onto the railway station. "It must be true."

Gyula did not answer. He still refused to let himself hope. Not until the last prisoners were bundled into the cattle cars and the whistle blew and the train chugged off with the heavy doors still wide open did he believe.

"It is true," he whispered to himself. "The war is over."

Freedom at Last

"You're the last one home, Gyula." Mama kissed him on both cheeks and cried and kissed him again. "I never thought I'd see you again. Nearly two years the war has been over!"

Gyula smiled and looked around the kitchen. Everything was as he remembered it—the old, scarred table in the center of the room, the heavy black kettle hissing a welcome. Papa and Mama a little older and gray haired. Laszlo and Mariska both grown taller.

But Istvan, poor Istvan. How thin and sick he looked.

Mama caught Gyula's gaze. "He was a prisoner-of-war in France," she explained, raising her voice to be heard above the welcoming din. "He's been home for more than a year, but his health doesn't improve."

Andras looked fat and healthy, but hadn't he been a prisoner-of-war too? Then how—? He raised his eyebrows at his brother.

"In an American camp," Andras grinned at Gyula.

For a few days Gyula enjoyed the luxury of having Mama feed him and fuss over him.

"How thin you are," she mourned. "My poor, poor boy. And your cough is terrible to hear. Oh, this dreadful, dreadful war. The bombing has stopped, but nothing will ever be the same again."

Mama hurried around the kitchen peeling this, chopping that. Mama had a gift with food. She could prepare a tasty something out of almost nothing.

And that was what everyone had to do nowadays. Gyula learned. Before the war Hungary had produced in one year sufficient food to last for four years. But all that had changed. First

Hitler robbed the country to feed his troops. Then Russia ravaged the land and the Hungarians themselves almost starved. Now the war was over but food was still scarce and black-market prices soared, despite the government controls.

For eighteen happy months the Nagy family enjoyed peace and a minimum of prosperity. All the brothers and Mariska had jobs. Papa and Mama managed the market stall. Everyone worked hard, but that was a way of life.

Then Laszlo turned twenty-one, and the government remembered his birthday with a call-up for a military service card. A few days later Gyula received his call-up.

"I guess they couldn't find me when I turned twenty-one," he flipped the printed summons over in his hands. "I was in the Ukraine."

Gyula's three years of compulsory service removed any doubts he had about his country's governmental leanings. Although his assignment of teaching new recruits to drive carried a certain amount of prestige, he had to attend meetings with the rest and listen to large daily doses of Communist propaganda.

Afterward, when the other youths congregated to argue about politics and parties and insisted that he give an opinion, Gyula's natural reticence stood him in good stead. He merely spread his hands in a noncommital gesture and shrugged. He had his own ideas as to where his country was headed, but not for anything would he put them into words.

After his stint as driving instructor Gyula transferred to airplane spotting and spent many happy months in a country-based unit identifying aircraft.

Next Gyula drove an army commandant's car, and this promotion suited him admirably. It meant frequent excursions into the country and many nights that he could spend at home, enjoying Mama's cooking and sleeping in his own warm bed.

In December 1951, shortly before he finished with the army, Gyula developed pneumonia and spent the holiday season in a military hospital. But in January he received his discharge from both hospital and army. It was time he had a change of scene.

"I've spent most of my working life at the Ford Motor Company," he said to Laszlo. "It's a fine place to work, but I think I've gone as high as I can go in their workshop. I think I'd like a change."

"Why don't you try the State Carrying Corporation where Istvan works? He's been there for years and seems happy with it."

Gyula joined the corporation and remained on their workforce for four years. But they were not happy years.

In 1956 Budapest reeled under the impact of student revolt. Unemployed, poverty-stricken, freedom-loving people joined them in resorting to violence. But the Nagy brothers kept out of it. They wanted nothing to do with politics on either side.

"Just let us get back to the old days," Mama said and wept when she heard details of the carnage in the streets. "We were poor then, yes, but we did not kill one another."

For a while after the smoke of civil battle cleared away, it seemed that Hungary was in for better days. But in a very short time the government changed again. A Russian puppet took charge and made no secret of his loyalties. "Anyone who doesn't like our system can put on his hat and get out," he shouted in a public meeting that the press reported.

All right, I will, Gyula said to himself and started planning his escape. Three years before it would have been impossible because minefields protected the Hungarian borders. Anyone caught inside the twenty-kilometer boundary risked death. But now the mines had been cleared away.

"I'll go with you," Laszlo said when Gyula confided his plans. "There's no future for us here. I know others who are going."

"So do I. But we'd better not let Mama and Papa know our plans. It will be safer for them to know nothing. We can write to them once we're safe."

"There'll be eight of us," Laszlo reported next day. "Andras wants to come and his wife and little girl, and three of my workmates."

"The more there are the greater the risk—especially the child."

Gyula sighed. "Tell them to take only what they can carry easily. We may have a lot of walking to do."

On the chosen day Laszlo and Gyula set off for the railway with large cloth bags slung over their shoulders. Out of the corner of his eye Gyula saw Andras and his family waiting on the platform. A little farther along Laszlo's elbow in his ribs told him that the workmates were there too. He made no sign. Time enough to meet together at day's end when they'd traveled as far as possible by rail.

Excitement, or was it fear, quickened Gyula's heartbeats as he and Laszlo got off the train at the designated station and went in search of a car to take them to their carefully selected village.

"Sure, I'll take you," a bearded old fellow winked knowingly and indicated an ancient six-seater. "If you can all fit in there."

Gyula nodded and paid the fare he asked. Laszlo shepherded the rest of the group along, and they and their baggage squeezed aboard.

The first fifteen kilometers passed without incident and Gyula's heart resumed its normal beat. So far so good. But, suddenly rounding a bend in the icy road they saw a guardhouse and a patrolling Hungarian officer stepped out of the guardhouse and held up his hand.

"Where are you off to?" he barked.

No one answered. Fear paralyzed their tongues.

"You're defectors, aren't you?" he shouted at them. "Traitors. Rats deserting to the West."

Gyula nodded wordlessly. It would be useless trying to deny it.

The officer's face reddened. For what seemed like hours he glared at them. Suddenly he raised his arm and crashed the battered mudguard with his fist. "Go then," he roared, "and good riddance to the likes of you."

The driver did not need to have the order repeated. With grinding gears he rattled off into the gathering dusk. Not long after, they arrived in the village. As he alighted Gyula gained the distinct impression that the inhabitants were accustomed to seeing defectors to the West arrive.

The others had scarcely tumbled out of the car and thanked the bearded driver before another whiskered individual sidled up to Andras.

"You want to cross?" he whispered. Andras pointed him to Gyula.

"Yes." Gyula drew him into the seclusion of the group. "Can you arrange it?"

"It is costly." The old man's eyes narrowed. "You have money?"

"A little." For a few minutes they dickered over the price. Then the old man pocketed the money Gyula gave him. "I'll come for you about eleven. The moon will be set then. Make sure that you are ready," he said as he shuffled away.

Gyula nodded. "We'll be waiting in the inn."

The hours dragged slowly by. Only Andras's small daughter slept. The others sat wrapped in apprehensive silence.

Laszlo's watch showed three minutes to the hour when a faint rapping on the window told them that the guide had arrived. The group shouldered their bundles, and Andras lifted the sleeping child in his arms. "Please, God, let her stay asleep," his wife muttered and crossed herself devoutly.

"Remember, no sound." Outside the inn the guide whispered his rapid instructions and then led the way through the sleeping village and out into the open fields. They walked in single file, silent as shadows.

Starlight reflecting from the snow enabled each one to see the shadowy form of the person directly in front of him. Hours, not miles, marked their onward progress. An icy wind despised their heavy overcoats and chilled them to the bone.

Abruptly the man in front stopped and the rest of the group drew up behind him. What was the matter? Had something gone wrong? Gyula strained his eyes to see ahead. Gradually he made out the darker mass of an unillumined guard tower. His heart pounded. This was it. This was the border.

The guide had warned them that army trucks patrolled at twenty-minute intervals. He looked around. There were no trees, no bushes, nothing to hide behind. The man in front of him dropped full length into the snow and Gyula followed suit.

Presently his straining ears caught the drone of an approaching motor. It came nearer—nearer. Its probing headlights pierced the night and Gyula held his breath. Surely they would be seen. Surely—

The terror passed. The group struggled upright and floundered forward, stumbling, sinking in the deep snow, gasping in their frantic endeavor to reach safety before the next patrol.

Every rasping breath, every swishing footstep thundered in Gyula's ears. Surely the guards inside the tower must hear? They had no dogs—the guide said they had no dogs—but—

He staggered on. Could eternity be longer than this? The man in front of him halted, and Gyula, head down against the wind, bumped into him.

"The guide's going back." Word passed down the line. "He says we're safe. We're in Austria now. Look ahead."

Gyula looked. The lights of a distant town flickered in the frosty air.

The group separated next morning. Each had his own ideas of what he wanted to do, where he wanted to go. Gyula and Laszlo changed some of their Hungarian money into Austrian schillings and purchased bus tickets to Vienna.

The journey took up most of the day, but what did it matter? They were free. For the first time in many years Gyula's heart filled with hope. Was it only his imagination, or did the sun shine more brightly in Austria than it did at home?

At dusk the bus chugged into the terminal and everyone alighted. The brothers claimed their paltry luggage and wandered out onto the city streets. What should they do now?

"The police," Laszlo suggested. "We don't have to be afraid of them here."

A man and a woman passed by, chatting to each other in Hungarian. Laszlo stopped them and asked for directions.

"Ah, you have just arrived? Good. The police station? Two

streets ahead and turn left. You won't miss the sign outside."

"Yes. Come in." A smiling officer welcomed the brothers. "You are refugees, yes? We have many refugees. You can selep here; in the morning you will be registered and taken to a camp."

A camp? Gyula froze. Laszlo saw his reaction and nudged him confidently. "This one will be different," he assured.

And it was. With their gray identification cards tucked safely in their pockets the brothers explored the school that had been turned over to the refugees. Bunk beds with plenty of blankets, hot water, towels, ample food, trousers, shirts, shoes. All for free. Gyula pinched himself. If this is what the bourgeois west was like, it would do for him.

For a day or two they rode the trams and got to know the city. Stephensplatz with its great cathedral, the old Hofburg Palace, the Lainzer Tiergarten zoo. Their gray tickets entitled them to free travel. When hunger overtook them they lined up at the International Committee for Refugees and received chicken soup, oranges, chocolate.

Ah, if only Mama could see them now. "This is a wonderful place," they wrote. "Everyone is so kind to us. We have everything we need. Presently we shall have to move on, but in the meantime—"

Both Gyula and Laszlo found employment in a shoe factory. The job carried no prestige, but it made them feel less dependent. Now they could at least pay their way while they waited for something to happen. The brothers still slept at Dadlergasse, and one cold night disaster struck.

An old Hungarian inmate came in long after everyone else slept. Flushed with liquor he crept to the nearest window and opened it wide. Gyula, sleeping directly underneath, did not stir. He did not feel the chilling blast until in the morning he awoke half-frozen.

Within a few days Gyula developed pneumonia, and the camp doctor sent him to a sanitorium on the outskirts of the city.

This time the examinations and treatments were so thorough that they frightened him. Had he contracted tuberculosis? What if he could not pass the immigration's medical tests? What if he had to return to Hungary because no other country would take him?

Gyula lay in bed tormented by a hundred fears. One afternoon two well-dressed gentlemen approached his bed and now he felt sure he would hear the worst. They were probably government officials come to tell him that he had failed the health requirements and that no other country would accept him. His heart sank.

"Good afternoon," he managed only a whispered reply to their greeting.

"We have come—" one man spoke and the other interpreted his words into Hungarian. Gyula only half listened. He did not want to hear. This was the end of all his hopes. The crumbling of all his castles in the air.

Suddenly a word arrested his attention.

"Delighted—we would be delighted if you would consider settling in Sweden. We need skilled tradesmen and you—"

Gyula sat bolt upright. "Then I'm well? I can work?"

"Yes, of course." The interpreter looked at the papers in his hand. "Your X rays show badly scarred lungs, but the sanitorium report says you are cleared. In a few days you can leave here."

"Thank you." A broad smile crept slowly across Gyula's face. "Thank you. I will talk it over with my brother and let you know."

"No, not Sweden." Laszlo shook his head and Rachel, sitting by his side with her arm tucked through his, said, "I want to go to America."

Much had happened while Gyula was in the hospital. Lonely at his leaving and lured by the glowing reports in his family letters, Laszlo's girlfriend had followed him into Austria. Now they were married and living in the couples' quarters at Dadlergasse.

Gyula shrugged. "Everyone wants to go to America."

The brothers went to see the harrassed officials handling the refugees' requests for America. He showed them the huge pile of papers on his desk. "All waiting for quotas and work opportunities in the United States," he said. "Why don't you apply for somewhere else? What about Australia? There's plenty of scope for young men there.''

Once they decided on Australia things happened fast. In an amazingly short time the three were transferred to a camp in Salzburg to learn English. Two weeks of concentrated classes and then they went by train to Marseilles in France, there to board an American troop ship, the *Harry Taylor* bound for the South Pacific.

Hundreds of refugees crowded onto the old troop carrier, and Captain Feher, an Hungarian-born American, arranged for English-language classes, and orientation lectures and question-and-answer periods. But when they arrived in Australia nothing had prepared the new arrivals for the easy-going ''She'll be right, mate'' attitude of their new countrymen. Fear found no foothold in this fair country. Except indirectly, war had never touched these golden shores.

Ten days in Greta refugee camp and the brothers each found work. Laszlo and Rachel settled in Sydney, and a visiting Hungarian foreman whisked Gyula off to the Port Kembla steel works near Wollongong.

''It's a fine place, this Australia,'' the foreman said as they sped along the highway, ''but you have to work hard. You must learn English quickly. Australians have no patience with anyone who can't understand their language.''

''I'll learn.'' Gyula settled back in the comfortable car seat and sighed his contentment. ''I'll work hard too. Someday I'll own a garage in this country.''

Ilona Balog

The year before Gyula Nagy squalled his way into the world in the village of Harsny, a family in the village of Ullo, some thirty kilometers from Budapest, expected another baby.

There were no excited speculations as to whether the baby would be a boy or a girl. No endlessly clicking knitting needles, no fashioning dainty wee garments for the new arrival.

After all, by the time she had produced thirteen boys and girls and fed and clothed them all, Mama Balog had plenty of hand-me-downs for the next one. There wasn't any need at all to be excited about the arrival of number fourteen, particularly when the mother was forty-four years old and hoping that this one would definitely be the last.

Not that Mama Balog did not love children—she did, and so did Papa Balog. When the tiny baby arrived they welcomed her as warmly as if there never had been and never again would be such an adorable baby. Never mind that all of the others had been equally as perfect, equally as adorable. This one was special—she was the newest, the very latest edition. All the other brothers and sisters gathered around to admire her and exclaim over her tiny hands and shell-like ears. They named her Ilona.

Ilona remembers now that as she grew up their house seemed always to be filled with love and laughter and children. Not all Balog children, of course, because some of the older siblings were already married and gone from the nest by the time Ilona put in her appearance.

Indeed, so she has since been told, shortly after she was born

49

her oldest sister, Anushka, produced a son. Because Anushka was unable to nurse him, Mama Balog came to the rescue and nursed baby Ilona and the grandson at alternate breasts.

"No wonder I'm so skinny," Ilona chided when she first heard the story. "You didn't feed me properly when I was a baby."

"Never mind, Helen, the most precious items are contained in the smallest parcels." Papa patted her head and drew her onto his knees for a comforting cuddle. Papa often called her Helen. He worked as a clerk in the American Embassy in Budapest, and he spoke English fairly well.

Mr. Balog was the envy of all the villagers because he received his salary in American dollars. Behind his back they called him "The Dollar King"; and the tradespeople vied with one another to change his dollars into Hungarian money—they could always manage to make a little on the deal. Besides it was most prestigious to have American money to flaunt in the faces of their relatives and friends.

Being the youngest and the last of the Balog tribe, everyone predicted that Ilona would be a spoiled darling. But this was not the case. Far from it, in fact. Being the youngest meant that the other thirteen all took it upon themselves to bring her up. Even John, three years older, and Kati, six years older, deemed it their privilege to order little sister about and even administer a quick slap if they felt she deserved it.

Despite all this Ilona has nothing but happy memories of her early childhood. In summer she played ball in the streets with the other village children or roamed the surrounding fields and lanes, gathering berries and wildflowers. In winter the family huddled cosily around the kitchen stove and listened to the wind whistling outside, while father raised his voice to read or to tell them stories.

Shortly before her seventh birthday, Ilona's beloved Papa became ill. "Pneumonia," the neighbors whispered and looked so serious and sad that Ilona's heart constricted with fear. What was pneumonia? Was it something as bad as the TB she often heard them mention? People with TB nearly always died—that's what they said.

The doctor came and went. Mama and the older girls seemed to spend most of their time in Papa's room ministering to his needs. No one had time to talk to Ilona or try to allay her fears about her Papa's condition.

Days dragged into weeks. Occasionally Papa felt a little better, and Ilona was allowed into his room to visit. The sight of him so pale and thin frightened her. This hollow-eyed stranger did not look at all like her darling Papa. She bravely took his hand and talked to him about school and how teacher was growing bulbs in pots on the windowsill so the children could watch them pushing their little green spikes through the soil.

Papa nodded and smiled. But when he tried to answer her, his voice sounded faint and wheezy. He began to cough and Mama hurried her outside and closed the door.

Then one day Ilona came home from school to find the house full of weeping people: older sisters and brothers with their husbands and wives, distant relatives, friends, neighbors. Mama in the center with John and Kati at her side, all red-eyed and blowing their noses.

For one dreadful moment she stood stricken, staring at them all. Then like a lightning flash she knew what had happened. "Papa," she shrieked and rushed past the outstretched, comforting hands, to throw herself on the bed and sob out her grief.

The embassy people were kindness itself. They allowed a suitable period for mourning to elapse and then sent one of their officials to visit Mrs. Balog with a proposition. Her husband had been one of their most valued employees, he said, and they were prepared to help his widow and her younger children. Did she want to accept a small pension for life, or would she prefer that the embassy employ two of her sons?

It did not take Mama Balog long to decide. Of course it would be better for her sons to have regular work; they were young. She, herself was past fifty, and who knew? If they had good jobs her sons would help with the younger children and provide for her in her old age. Yes, yes, of course it would be best to provide employment for two of the boys.

But things did not work out quite as well as that. While the sons lived at home all went well. But when they married and moved into homes of their own the daughters-in-law resented Mama Balog's dependence. There were so many things that they themselves needed to set up housekeeping. Every dollar must be stretched to the limit—things were *so* expensive.

Mama Balog refused to be a burden to anyone. She wanted no reluctant charity. "It's all right," she told her sons. "Your duty is to your wives. Don't worry about me, I'll manage."

But Mama Balog had no trade or profession to fall back on. Almost all of her life had been spent in keeping house and raising children, and every other woman in the village did *that*. She decided to ask around among the farmers for work.

But even farm work was not easily come by. Mama inquired here and there and eventually she heard of a farmer who needed an extra hand for the grape harvest. She tramped the three kilometers out of town to his vineyard.

Yes, he could employ her on the same conditions as he employed the younger women, a quarter of a forint for each basket of grapes picked. She must be careful not to drop the bunches or squeeze them; they were for the market. Did she know a ripe grape when she saw one? Some pickers didn't. Unripe grapes were sour, and if they were mixed in with the others that would spoil his reputation.

After the grapes came the carrots. Rows and rows of them that had to be carefully dug and washed and then bunched. Again her employer issued directives: Put some small ones in with the big ones. Put them in the center so they won't be noticed. Bunch them tightly together and tie the tops with a stem of twisted grass before you put them on the wheelbarrow. Like this, see?

Mama's back ached and her legs swelled. Her work-roughened hands cramped from hours of grasping spade or hoe. Often at night she could scarcely straighten her fingers. But she kept up with, and often outstripped, many of the younger women working beside her.

Most of these women lived close by, and when their working

day ended they trudged home to a clean house and a hot meal prepared by some live-in aunty or mother-in-law.

But no such luxury awaited Mama. After work she dragged her tired body those endless kilometers home to prepare food, wash, iron, scrub, or tackle any of the thousands of other tasks that awaited her.

It was the same in the mornings. Long before dawn she arose and tucked a thick crust of bread into her apron pocket, drank a hasty cup of coffee, and set out on her long walk. Ilona and John got their own breakfast and went off to school, and Kati caught the city train to work.

Of course they helped their mother too. Mama saw to that. But they had school lessons to prepare, and there were always a dozen and one reasons or excuses as to why they did not do more. Kati left home too early—she arrived back too late. And besides, she worked as a bookbinder in a printing establishment in the city. It sounded like an important position, but actually, at least to begin with, it was a low rung on the publishing ladder. But Kati did not mind. She enjoyed the independence of earning her own salary, small as it was, and meeting different people, and making new friends.

Kati Balog sang like a nightingale; all the villagers said so. All through her schooldays no concert or gala event was complete unless Kati Balog was featured on the program. The nuns at the convent predicted a great future for her if she had her voice trained. But there was no money for such a luxury as that; a few lessons here and there and plenty of practice in the choir—that was the most that Kati could hope for.

About the time that Ilona reached her twelfth year Kati developed stomach pains. Mama tried all the usual home remedies: hot packs and purgatives and lukewarm salt water to make her vomit in case it was something that she'd eaten. But the pain persisted. In fact it grew stronger and Kati cried and groaned so much that Mama became frightened and called in the doctor.

"Hmm, it could be appendicitis," the doctor said, and gave Mama a letter to take along with Kati to a city hospital.

Appendicitis! Kati swelled with importance at the very idea. Appendicitis meant an operation, and an operation meant a stay in the hospital, and a stay in hospital meant ever so many interesting and exciting things could happen. Appendicitis! Why, she'd be the talk of the village, the envy of all the other girls. And the scar it would leave. Kati's excitement quite eclipsed her pain.

Appendicitis it was, and as soon as a bed became available Kati was admitted to Stephen's Hospital in Budapest. Mama fretted because she would not be able to visit Kati very often, what with work and the high cost of fares. But Ilona traveled half price; she could go every day or so.

"Never mind, never mind." Kati dismissed Mama's worries with an airy wave. "I'll be all right. The sisters are wonderfully kind, so I've heard, and the doctors—" her voice trailed off into daydreams.

"How do you feel now, dear?" The woman in the next bed leaned forward when she saw Kati's eyelids flutter.

"I'm—all—right." Kati's swollen tongue seemed to fill her mouth. Her words sounded thick and strange in her ears. "I'd—like—a drink."

"I'll call a nurse for you." The older woman picked up a small handbell on her locker and shook it vigorously.

Kati tried desperately to focus on the woman, on the locker, on anything; but by the time the bell's faint tinkle summoned a nurse she had fallen asleep again.

Next day Kati felt ever so much better. Her head wasn't pumpkin-sized anymore and she saw one woman in the next bed instead of two.

"I'm Irna, Irna Kisz," the woman introduced herself when she saw Kati's eyes open. "I live in Budapest, and I've had a gallstone operation."

"I'm Kati Balog and I come from Ullo." Kati raised herself on her elbow and ended proudly, "I had my appendix taken out."

From that point the friendship progressed rapidly. With little else to do but visit, the two talked for hours on end, exchanging confidences, relating family histories, swapping anecdotes. Soon Kati learned that her new friend was a Seventh-day Adventist.

"A Seventh-day what?" she asked. The first two words were familiar enough but she'd never heard of an Adventist.

"Adventist. A Seventh-day Adventist. It means that we believe in the second advent, the second coming of Christ to this world."

"Oh?" said Kati.

"Yes, and the Seventh-day part means that we worship God on the seventh day of the week instead of the first. We attend church on Saturday, not on Sunday."

"Oh," Kati said again. This was the strangest thing she'd ever heard. Perhaps she'd better be careful. Irna seemed such a lovely person, but one never knew. As soon as she got home again she'd ask Mama whether she had ever heard of any religion like that.

"Do you know the Ten Commandments?" Irna broke into Kati's thoughts.

"Yes, we learned them at catechism."

"Good. Then you know that the fourth commandment says to keep holy the seventh-day."

"Yes, but that means Sunday. Everyone goes to church on Sunday."

"That doesn't make it the *right* day. You look on a calendar. Sunday is the *first* day of the week; Saturday is the *seventh.*"

"Yes, but—"

The discussions went on and on; hour by hour, day after day. Irna Kisz seemed able to quote a Bible text that silenced every objection that Kati raised. And not only on the subject of which day to keep holy—they discussed life after death and heaven and hell and purgatory; any religious topic that came up Irna could talk about it.

And the prophecies! She kept Kati enthralled for hours reading to her from the worn Bible she kept on her bedside locker and explaining as she read.

"The lion with eagle's wings means the same nation as the head of gold that King Nebuchadnezzar saw in his dream. Remember, I told you about Daniel 2 yesterday?"

"Yes," Kati nodded vigorously. Her polite listening had long since changed to real live interest. By the time the doctor pronounced her incision healed and discharged her from the hospital she had promised to go along to visit Irna Kisz's church as soon as she felt strong enough. Her discovery of this wonderful new religion quite eclipsed the importance of her operation.

"And you may come with me," Kati told Ilona. In fact, since her return from the hospital Kati talked of little else but Irna Kisz and her church, her Bible, and all the wonderful things that Irna had told her.

Young John scoffed and teased. "Kati's got religion, Kati's got religion," he chanted over and over. "Now she's going to be a saint and go to church on Saturday. A mad saint. A mad saint. Ha! Ha! Ha!

Poor Mama Balog. She often wished that Papa was back to help her raise these last three children. At fifteen John needed a father's strong hand. He was always wanting to be out with the other boys, and who knew what they got up to when a crowd of them ran around together.

And now Kati was all taken up with this new friend and her strange ideas. An older woman too. Mama sighed. Well, at least she could be thankful that it was religion that had caught Kati's fancy and not some of these other dreadful crazes that some of the young folk followed.

"Yes, you may go." Mama nodded assent when Ilona asked permission to attend the Saturday church with Kati. "Keep close to your sister; don't go wandering off anywhere by yourself, or you might get lost in the big city."

And that, Mama said to herself, cuts both ways. If Ilona keeps close by Kati, then Kati won't have a chance to get into mischief either.

For several months Ilona attended Saturday services with Kati. Occasionally there were middle-of-the-week meetings too, prayer circles and rallies and special occasions when Ilona sat proudly in her seat and listened to her big sister holding the congregation enthralled with her lovely voice. But after a while Kati found the traveling back and forth to work and meetings too tedious and time consuming, and she left home and went to board with some of her Seventh-day Adventist friends in the city.

Ilona missed the warm-hearted fellowship of the church on Szecej Bertilan Ucca and sometimes talked to her mother about the things that she had heard there. "I'd like to go back to that church someday," she said. Mama looked distressed and wished aloud that her daughters would be content to remain good Roman Catholics as their father had been, and his parents, and their parents, and so on right back to who knows when. To say nothing of her own side of the family—good staunch Catholics all of them.

Ilona said nothing. There were too many other things to worry about at present. Mama's health for instance. Mama never complained, but sometimes she dragged herself home from work and went straight to bed, completely ignoring the washing and ironing and all the other tasks that needed to be done—and that was so unlike Mama. At other times she had caught Mama with her arms folded across her stomach and groaning with pain.

"It's nothing," she said when Ilona, pale and frightened, wanted to call the doctor. "Just indigestion. Must be something I've eaten." Then she mixed herself a dose of bismuth and dropped into bed.

As well as worrying about Mama, Ilona had her own future to worry about. In a month or two she'd be finished with school, and then what would she do? There were no jobs available in the village, and not many in the city, especially right now with this madman Hitler roaring up and down Germany and everyone nervously wondering whether he really *could* set Europe on fire.

Should she take a secretarial course or go out to service in the city or maybe look for an apprenticeship? Her friend, Susie, was apprenticed to a tailor. Should she look for something like that too?

Mama finally made the decision for her.

"I've heard of a dressmaking establishment in Pest—Madame Irene Fashions. Madame takes girls and teaches them sewing and cutting and all the rest." Mama eased her work-bent body into the kitchen rocker and looked up at Ilona with pain-filled eyes. "She's a relative of one of the women who digs carrots with me. She'll give us an introduction."

Not long after Ilona began her dressmaking apprenticeship Anushka, her older sister, persuaded Mama to consult the village doctor. He listened to her reluctant description of her symptoms, examined her, and then shook his head gravely. This was something far beyond his capabilities.

"You'll have to see a specialist in the city," he said. "I'll give you a letter."

The specialist was kind enough, but cool and businesslike. After all, Mama Balog meant nothing special to him; she was just another one of the hundreds of careworn men and women who passed through his clinic. He insisted on X rays and tests of all kinds. When Mama and Anushka came to find out the results, he came straight to the point.

"Cancer," he said. "Impossible to estimate its extent until we operate."

Cancer! The diagnosis threw the whole family into a turmoil. There was no question of Mama going back to work—ever. Thank God the family were all grown and self-supporting, even Ilona. Well, she would be in a year or two when she finished her course; in the meantime they'd somehow manage her food and fares.

Anushka and her family moved into the old Balog home to care for Mama when she came home from the hospital. The rest of the family rallied around and did what they could to make Mama's last days happy ones. They *knew* that her days were numbered even though the specialist used a lot of important-sounding words and unintelligible scientific terms when they asked him the result of the surgery.

She lived for two years after her operation. Her family watched helplessly as she grew thinner and weaker and finally took to her bed. One day, toward the end, when Kati was visiting her, Mama opened her tired eyes and looked directly at Kati.

Kati immediately sensed that Mama wanted to say something. "Yes, Mama, what is it?" she bent her head to catch Mama's words.

"Do you think," Mama whispered, "that your—minister— would visit—me?"

"I'm sure he will, Mama, I'm sure he will." Kati choked and tenderly kissed her mother's pale cheek. "I'll ask him this very night."

There were tears in Kati's eyes and a song in her heart. All those years Mama had been listening after all.

Rape or Murder?

Mama's death marked the total collapse of Ilona's small world. Now she had nothing to cling to, no anchor. John had long since been drafted into the army. Kati joined the secret police, optimistically expecting to combine religious convictions with loyalty to her country. All the rest of the brothers and sisters had their own families to think about. Susie, her dear friend of childhood days, now lived a long way out on the other side of the city. During the week they usually met at the railway station and visited awhile before catching their respective trains; but now that she had completed her course at Madame Irene's, Ilona didn't know what was going to happen.

"I'll have to find work," she told herself, "and that isn't going to be easy. Susie finished her tailoring course months ago, and she hasn't found a job yet."

Of course Ilona could stay on in the family home with Anushka and her husband and girls. One of the nieces was older than Ilona, and two were younger; Anushka treated them all equally. Just the same Ilona felt the need to become independent; it wasn't fair to her brother-in-law, poor man, having an extra mouth to feed. Fortunately he was older and had not been taken off into the army like all the young men in the village. But still life wasn't easy for any of them.

Periodically Ilona and the other girls went through their wardrobes searching for clothing that could be spared to barter for food. Farmers' wives were glad to give eggs and butter or chickens and meat in exchange for fashionable city wear.

But there was a limit to the clothing that they could spare, and it seemed to Ilona that she was always hungry. Sometimes at night she dreamed of the bountiful meals that they had enjoyed long ago when Papa was alive—before this dreadful war—while Mama— and then she would awake to find her pillow wet with tears.

Ilona's comfort during these trying times was her Bible, the one that Kati had given to Mama. No one else had wanted it, so Ilona claimed it and kept it with her as a kind of sacred talisman. She rarely opened the covers; it was too hard to understand. She rarely prayed, but deep in her heart she believed. She knew that God was there, and she turned to Him in times of trouble.

Ilona and her friend Susie sat side by side in the depot on one of their few meetings. Ilona had just been to see about a job.

"She said she'd let me know when a vacancy occurs." Ilona shrugged and her mouth twisted into a sardonic smile. "They all say the same thing though."

Susie sighed. "Mmm, they all blame it on the war. They say there's no demand for fashion sewing in such serious times. I suppose it's true, but you'd think the employment office could find us some kind of work."

Armed with the daily newspapers the two girls had spent the day job hunting in Budapest. As a last resort they had tried the government employment agency. Now they lingered in the bustling station before catching their separate trains.

Ilona usually traveled by tram because it was cheaper, but today Susie had suggested that she go by train. "It will give us longer to talk," she insisted. "You always leave so early when you travel by tram."

"You know that's because of the long walk at the other end," Ilona protested. "My sister says I must—"

"Yes, I know—" Susie paused as the doors of a nearby theater opened, and a mixed stream of servicemen and aged civilians poured across the street. "Lucky things."

"Lucky all right," Ilona agreed. "I wish I could afford the price of a meal, let alone a theater ticket. I'm starving."

As if they had heard her remark, two young men left the crowd and approached the girls. One stood tall and lean and was dressed in civilian clothes; the other, slightly shorter, wore the uniform of a Russian officer, complete with holstered pistol. The one in civilian clothes walked right up to Ilona and grinned engagingly. "You girls in a hurry?"

Ilona looked at Susie. Susie had been around more than she had. Susie had two brothers still at home, and she was used to handling them.

Susie smiled back a little warily. "Not really."

"Fine. Then how about taking pity on a couple of country boys. We don't know any girls here. How'd you like to eat with us? Are you hungry?"

Hungry? Ilona and Susie exchanged ravenous glances. Wartime rations were never enough for their youthful appetites. Besides today had been worse than usual. Neither of them had eaten a bite since early morning. Surely it would be all right, their eyes telegraphed to each other. It was still only four o'clock. And the young man in civilian clothes was obviously Hungarian; he spoke like a villager.

"What about your friend?" Susie put the question. "He's a Russian, isn't he?"

The young man waved an airy assurance. "Sure, he's Russian, but I can vouch for him. Real fine fellow, Ivan, not his fault he's an enemy. In fact he's the one that suggested we speak to you." He nodded at Ilona. "He said you reminded him of his sister."

Ilona relaxed. Surely any young man—even a Russian—with a sister would be all right; he'd treat them courteously. Her eyes mirrored her relief and Susie took the cue.

"All right," she said, "But we mustn't be late getting home."

"Let's take a tram to Buda; a friend of mine has a little cafe halfway up the hill." The young man led the way and politely handed the girls onto the tram. Soon all four had exchanged names and were laughing and chatting like old friends. Even Ivan, whose knowledge of Hungarian was as sparse as the girls' knowledge of Russian, managed to converse with signs and shrugs and facial expressions.

The tram rattled through the business section of Pest, crossed the Danube, and banged its way along the old streets of Buda. Ilona nodded to herself as they approached various magnificent old spired buildings, focused briefly, and then left them behind. She knew this part of the city fairly well. Her brother Viktor lived on Isten Hegyi Ut, the long street where many consulates and embassies housed their staff.

"Here we are." Nikolas, the Hungarian, swung himself down and helped the girls to alight. "There's the cafe." He pointed to a scatter of tables and chairs half hidden by great masses of greenery in red and yellow tubs. "Sit down. I'll tell Otto we're here."

They sat down and Ilona's stomach gurgled with anticipation. Food. Nikolas called for plates and knives and white-bread rolls. Ivan produced tins of meat from his capacious pockets. "Let's have some wine." Nikolas snapped his fingers and, an ancient waiter brought a bottle and glasses.

"No, thank you." Ilona refused but Nikolas poured it into her glass anyway. She took a sip and when he wasn't looking she emptied the rest into the nearest tub. Behind Ivan's back Susie did the same with hers.

"Come on, girls, eat as much meat as you want." Ivan spread his arms expansively, and Nikolas translated his gesture. "He can get plenty more; the army isn't rationed."

Ilona needed no urging. Months, or was it years, of privation had to be made up as she chewed on white bread and meat. Meat. What a change from rye and turnips. When the last bite had been swallowed, she wiped her mouth and looked at Nikolas.

"Thank you so much. We had better be going back to the station now."

"Oh, no hurry; no hurry. We'll take you back in a tram. Let's go for a walk up the mountain."

"We really shouldn't, it's—" Ilona protested uneasily and turned to Susie for support, but Susie had her head bent and was concentrating on something that Ivan said.

So the four set off, still joking and talking as they passed stately homes and elegant gardens, down one street and up another. Ilona noted that their wanderings had brought them close to a wooded section only a block or so from Isten Hegyi Ut. "My brother lives out here." She halted to speak to Susie who was strolling along with Ivan. As she did so Nikolas dropped behind and spoke in a low voice to Ivan. They appeared to argue about something.

Fear stabbed at Ilona's heart. "Susie," she grabbed her friend's arm and walked rapidly up the hill. "Susie, we must go—get back to the station."

"I know. But how to get rid of them now? We really shouldn't have—"

Breathing heavily, the young men caught up with them. "Come on, let's take a walk through the woods." There was a new gruffness in Nikolas's voice as he took Ilona's arm and tried to steer her toward the park.

"No. It is getting late. Thank you for a pleasant outing, but we must return to Pest. My sister will worry."

"Don't be a fool," Nikolas rasped. "Why do you think we spent our money on you?"

Ilona's knees turned to jelly. Out of the corner of her eye she saw that Susie was trying unsuccessfully to shake Ivan off—they were headed in the direction of the woods. Oh dear, what should she do? The darkening streets were almost deserted now. Should she scream? Try to run? No, better try to act natural. Ilona's legs trembled and agonized prayers throbbed in her mind: "God, please help us. I didn't know—truly I didn't know. Oh, forgive me for being so stupid. Help me. I was *so* hungry."

Again Nikolas tried to urge her aside into a small park but Ilona hurried ahead, forcing him to accompany her. "No, no. I know a better place."

"Where?"

Ilona pointed. "A little further. Just a little further."

If only she could keep him walking until they reached Viktor's place. "Please God, help. Help Susie too." Susie and Ivan had long since disappeared. What was happening to Susie? Ilona shuddered and renewed her prayers. "Please save us, Please—"

Suddenly behind them a single shot shattered the suburban silence. Ilona swung around. "What's that?"

Her whole body shook with fear. She tried to peer back through the gathering gloom.

"Probably he's shot her," Nikolas grinned.

"Oh, no!" Ilona burst into tears.

"Shut up, you fool." Nikolas slapped her face. The fingers of his other hand bit into her arm as if to say, don't you try any funny business. "Come on, where's this good place of yours."

"A little further," Ilona sobbed and staggered forward. Through the dusk she saw the tall outline of the house next door to Viktor's. If only—another fifty paces. Please God—another thirty paces—

Another few steps and they'd be abreast of the gate. Ilona's heart pounded. With a supreme effort she wrenched herself free and tore down the path. "My brother lives here," she called over her shoulder and pounded on the front door. "Viktor, Viktor, let me in." Behind her she heard Nikolas's oaths.

"What's the matter? What's happened?" Ilona's sister-in-law opened the door and dragged the distraught girl inside.

"Susie's dead. That wicked man—" Ilona burst into a fresh flood of tears and sobbed out her story.

"It's a good thing for you that your brother is not home," her sister-in-law said harshly. "He would kill you for having anything to do with a Russian."

"But we didn't know," Ilona sobbed. "He spoke Hungarian like a native, and we were *so* hungry."

"He was probably a Secret Service man, a spy. Let this be a lesson to you. I'm sure that Susie is not dead, raped perhaps, but not dead."

Her sister-in-law's cold words did little to allay Ilona's fears. If Susie was alive, then what was the shot she had heard? All night she tossed and turned on her makeshift bed. Why had they done such a foolish thing? It was all her fault. She should have known better.

As soon as she had helped with the morning chores Ilona trudged back to Pest and caught the train to Ullo. As she expected, Anushka had been worried when she did not return home, and her anxiety increased tenfold when she heard Ilona's story.

"This is terrible," she cried. "What can we do? How can we find out about Susie?"

Ilona shook her head. They had no telephone; neither did Susie's folks. Telegrams were expensive and unreliable. She could write, but it would take days to receive a reply.

Suddenly Anushka jumped up and rummaged behind the cushions on the old-fashioned chair. "Here." She held out a small purse. "This is my emergency bank. Take this money for your train fares. Go straight back to the city. You know where Susie's father works, don't you?"

Ilona nodded and more tears coursed down her pale cheeks. "I can't face him," she whispered.

"You'll have to. We must know."

All the way back to the city Ilona trembled. She went straight to the place where Susie's father worked.

"No. He ain't here. Didn't come to work at all today," one of the workers told her.

"Thank you." Ilona's heart turned to stone. Her sister-in-law was wrong. Susie was dead. She had resisted Ivan's advances, and he had shot her. Ilona pictured the whole scene. How could she ever face Susie's parents? Her brothers? They would blame her, of course. Oh God, how terrible. She sobbed all the way home.

At last Ilona screwed up her courage and wrote to Susie's parents—a careful little note—telling nothing, asking only whether Susie was all right, she had looked a little pale the last time they'd met.

Imagine her surprise when Susie herself replied and suggested that they meet in the city at their usual place.

"What happened? Are you all right?" They threw themselves into each other's arms and sobbed with joy.

"Come over here and tell me about it," Ilona drew Susie toward a vacant bench on the railway platform.

"There isn't much to tell." Susie blew her nose and mopped at her eyes. "After you and Nikolas went on ahead Ivan pushed me in front of him into that wooded park alongside the road. I thought I'd better pretend to go along with him, so we sat down on the grass. He took off his hat and pistol holster. I stood up and unbuttoned my coat to make him think I was about to take it off. Then suddenly I grabbed his hat and slammed it down over his face and ran. I ran out to the street and I saw lights in a house and I ran in there and banged on the door. Fortunately the woman answered straight away. I quickly told her what had happened, and she took me in and hid me under the huge wooden tubs in her washroom.

"I scarcely had time to get my legs tucked in before I heard him pounding on the door and yelling, *'Barisnya! Barisnya!'*

"The woman opened the door and told him there was no girl there, and he could come in and search for himself. But he didn't. He went away cursing and muttering."

"Oh, Susie, it's a wonder he didn't catch you."

"Well, I can run fast. And he had to get the hat off his face first and pick up his gun and—"

"Maybe that's when he fired the shot I heard."

"I don't know. I didn't hear anything. I was too frightened."

"Anyway, thank God you're safe." Ilona raised her eyes heavenward.

"Thank God, we're both safe." Susie nodded solemnly.

Eventually Ilona found temporary work in Budapest at the same dress factory where her oldest niece was employed. Shortly afterward the whole family moved into Budapest.

"We'd be better off in the city," Anushka's husband said one day "I fear for the girls' safety out here. Those—those—beasts!"

War raged on every side. Not an able-bodied young Hungarian man remained in Ullo village. Russian soldiers swarmed over the countryside, and no one and no thing was safe from their depredations. Food and valuables mysteriously disappeared. Even in daylight women and girls went about in groups if they had to walk or work outside of their homes. One of Ilona's former schoolmates was caught and raped; the cruelty and humiliation of it left her insane. German-born Hungarians were rounded up and shipped off to prison camps in Siberia.

Surely this must be the "time of trouble" that she'd heard about at Kati's church. Ilona crossed herself and wondered anew about that mysterious "second coming of Christ." Was it about to happen?

Anushka's husband went ahead to find somewhere for them to live in Budapest. Soon he found a place, and the whole family moved into one of the city's grand old homes that had been divided into lodgings for half a dozen impoverished families.

For some months all went well; the youngest girl attended high school and the others all had jobs. But the big city did not provide the anonymity for which they craved.

One evening a thunderous knocking at the front door announced the presence of a Russian officer.

"You have some girls here?" he asked the quaking tenant who opened the door a crack.

To the answer, the officer replied, "I don't believe you. I will come back later and bring my men. We will search," he threatened and turned on his heel.

Panic swept through the lodging house as one tenant spread the word to another. "The Russians are coming back to look for girls."

"What can we do?" Anushka wrung her hands in anguish and looked from husband to daughters and back again.

"I don't know," he answered, his face ashen. "They've probably seen the girls going in and out. They can't escape. There's nowhere to hide."

"We'll pray." Teeth chattering with terror, Ilona grabbed her Bible before she and her nieces squirmed under Anushka's huge double bed. The thick coverlet hung to the floor. Surely it would be the first place the soldiers would look, but they had nowhere else to go.

Trembling with fear Ilona lay in the darkness, her ears strained to catch the slightest sound. Beside her the younger nieces clung together sobbing quietly. "Oh, save us, God," Ilona prayed under her breath. "Save us." She clutched her Bible to her heart and silently pleaded again and again. "Save us! Oh, please, save us!"

A muffled hammering at the front door sent her into a paroxysm of fear. "Oh, God, help us, save—Oh, save us!"

Almost unconscious with fright Ilona waited for the footsteps on the stairs, the harsh voices, the unceremonious snatching aside of the coverlet. An eternity passed. There was no sound.

Presently a corner of the coverlet was raised, and Anushka's voice whispered, "You can come out now. You're safe."

Emotionally exhausted Ilona crawled out of their hiding place and sat with her nieces at their mother's feet. "What happened? Where are the soldiers?"

Anushka wiped her eyes. Her husband blew his nose repeatedly. "You tell them," he choked, too overcome to talk.

"Only one Russian came, after all," Anushka wiped her eyes again. "The same officer. He banged at the door and no one opened it. Everyone was too frightened. He banged and yelled. Finally the woman from the front room opened the door. I don't know what she said, but they talked for a little while, and he laughed. Then she darted back into her room and got a coat, and they went off together."

"That woman," Ilona echoed. *"That* woman saved us?"

Not only their lodging house but the whole street knew of *her* doubtful reputation. Anyone consorting with a Russian was considered not only a whore but also a traitor to her country.

"I don't know whether she did it out of compassion for you girls," Anushka's husband said, "or whether she just wanted a night out."

"It doesn't matter." Ilona fingered her Bible reverently. "God used her to save us."

A Loveless Marriage

War's end restored a certain amount of normality to Hungarian life, but it made little difference to Ilona. She still felt lonely and unwanted. Susie, her friend and confidant, had married and though she had professed undying love for Ilona, things could never be the same again. Anushka and her family had moved back to Ullo, and Kati was here, there, and everywhere—touring Europe with an operatic company.

Ilona's brothers and sisters were all good to her, even the sisters-in-law, but they all had their own families and their own interests. She was the odd man out. If only Mama were alive. Often she sighed for the happy days that were forever gone.

The end of the war seemed to spell the end of Ilona's need for God. At twenty-two she thought little of God nor did she ever read her Bible now. She had a good, steady job; she lived in a pleasant enough rented room in the city—surely she was old enough and worldly-wise enough now to take care of herself.

It was while Ilona was in this stubbornly independent mood that a workmate introduced her to Charles. Charles was more than ten years older than she, already married, but living apart from his wife and two children.

"Where have you been all my life?" he demanded passionately when they were on their own. "If only we had met ten years ago, how different my life would have been."

Ilona fell for it. She had no one to warn her. This was what she had looked for all her life—well, the last four or five years at least—someone to love her, to cherish her, to treat her as if she were someone special. And Charles did all of these things well.

Their courtship progressed as happily and properly as Ilona had expected any courtship would. Oh, once or twice Charles was late for an appointment with her and several times she caught him talking to another girl, giving her money. But he always had a plausible explanation. He brought Ilona gifts too, delicious sponge cakes smothered in cream, and Swiss pastries. He said that one of the girls at his work made them. Once Ilona found a note underneath one of the cakes: "Sweets to the sweet, my darling Charles," but when she showed it to him he laughed it off and said it was only a joke.

Anushka did not like Charles. "He's a philanderer, you mark my words. Don't you ever marry him. He wouldn't be faithful to you for ten minutes."

Ilona paid no attention to Anushka's opinion. But she kept her eyes and ears open, and during the next eighteen months many of the scales fell from her eyes. Rumors of Charles's exploits with other women reached her and finally she had had enough.

"It's all off," she told him the next time he came to see her. "You are not faithful to me. I can't believe a word that you say. I'm not going to marry you, and I don't ever want to see you again."

Charles begged, cajoled, promised. Finally he threatened to commit suicide, but Ilona remained adamant. "No, our friendship is over."

"All right, if I can't have you no one else shall." He threw the words over his shoulder and stalked off in truly theatrical fashion.

Later that evening he came back again, and Ilona's unsuspecting, deaf old landlady showed him to her room.

"I've come to kill you." Charles closed the door behind him and drew a wicked-looking knife from under his coat.

Ilona's eyes widened in fear. This was a different side of Charles. How did she handle this?

"Don't play jokes," she said through dry lips. "Put that knife down."

"This is not a joke." He lunged forward.

Ilona dodged and screamed. "Don't, Charles, don't kill me." She cried hysterically and dropped in a sobbing heap at his feet begging for her life.

"All right." Charles sheathed his knife. "But no more of this monkey business. You're mine. I've courted you for nearly three years. As soon as my divorce is through we're being married. I won't be denied."

Eventually he left and Ilona feverishly began to pack her things. She'd leave this room—go someplace where Charles wouldn't find her. She opened drawers and closet and stuffed clothes willy-nilly into bags and suitcase. She'd leave early in the morning, as soon as it was light. She could write to her landlady afterward. The bulging suitcase refused to lock, and Ilona tied it shut with a stout string. She planned to take all her belongings to work with her. Surely one of the other women would be able to help her find a place to live.

And one of the women at work said, "I'm sure my landlady has a spare room. Come home with me this afternoon. There are about eighty of us lodgers. I'm sure she'll find you a corner."

After work the pair sneaked out a back door in case Charles was waiting out front. Between them they lugged Ilona's bulging suitcase and bags to her workmate's lodgings where they found a vacant room.

That very night Charles somehow found where Ilona had gone and forced his way into her room. "You can't escape me." His wild eyes searching the room fell on her suitcase. "I'll kill you this time."

Before Ilona could move, he had grabbed the cord from the suitcase and fashioned it into a noose.

"I'll choke you." Charles tried to slip the cord over her head but she fought him off, screaming for help.

"He's killing me. Help! Help!"

Doors flew open and lodgers rushed from all directions. Ilona wrenched herself free and tried to open the door. Charles slammed it on her hand.

"Police," a woman shrieked. "Call the police."

Eventually it was all sorted out without police intervention. Male lodgers rallied en masse and hustled Charles out of the building. Females crowded around Ilona offering sympathy and succour.

"My heart," the landlady gasped and clasped her hands to her ample bosom. "I have a bad heart." Gasping she sank onto a hall chair and looked at Ilona severely. "In all my years—all the hundreds of lodgers who've lived here—there's never been anything like this happen. You'll have to leave. Oh, my heart, my poor, poor heart."

"May I use your telephone?" Ilona tearfully asked. She lifted the receiver from its hook. She'd telephone her friend in Vesces village.

"I can't stay here," she sobbed after telling her friend all that had happened. "And I can't go to Anushka because Charles knows where she lives. I'll have to leave my job too. I—"

"I'll come for you in the morning," her friend promised.

The next morning Ilona once again knotted a cord around her battered suitcase, and the two girls lugged it across the city. They had almost reached the railway station when Charles fell into step beside her. He must have watched the house.

"Ilona, my darling, please listen to me," he said humbly. "I'm sorry I frightened you. I'm sorry I made such a scene. I was beside myself at the thought of losing you."

Ilona ignored him and kept on walking, eyes averted and head held high. Charles turned imploringly to her friend. "Tell her I love her. Please make her understand. I'll never do it again, never, never. I lost my head, that's all. I love her. She—"

They halted outside the station and Charles renewed his pleas.

"Well," Ilona's friend hesitated and looked from one to the other. "Maybe you—" She turned to Ilona, "Perhaps you should—"

For half an hour they stood outside the busy station and argued the matter back and forth. In the end it was decided that Charles would be given another chance.

"But this is the last time," Ilona warned. "And I'm staying in

Vesces with my friend. I can get some piecework to do." Her eyes conveyed her distrust.

"All right, I'll come and visit you there," Charles agreed.

And he did. Once or twice a week and on weekends he took the train to Vesces and concentrated on winning back Ilona's affections.

Some of Ilona's friends and relatives urged her to marry him. "He's a charming fellow, Ilona. Of course, he's sowed his wild oats no doubt, but he's paid the price. He'll settle down now. You'll see."

Others just as vehemently urged her not to marry him. "Don't even think of it, Ilona. Send him packing once and for all. He's got a roving eye, that one. I wouldn't trust him as far as the front gate."

Finally, "You're not getting any younger, Ilona," someone pointed out. "You mightn't find anyone else, and even though you're earning your way with your piecework, you can't live with your friend forever."

Early in May 1952 Ilona and Charles were married in a Budapest registry. They were so poor that they had no flowers, no finery; no friends came to wish them well. Indeed, the official had to call two passersby in from the street to witness their signing of the wedding document.

Charles had to pay alimony to his former wife, and all of Ilona's small savings went to put a deposit on the small apartment that they rented. One of Ilona's brothers gave her some of his excess furniture, other family members helped with this and that, and Ilona soon fashioned frilly drapes and trimmings for their little home.

In June Ilona found that she was pregnant.

"Oh no," she wailed, aghast at the prospect of motherhood so soon after becoming a wife. "We cannot have a baby. We have no money. I must work, and there is no one to mind the baby while I go to work."

In this crisis Ilona once again received conflicting advice. All her Roman Catholic friends and relatives were horrified at her protestations. They urged her to have the baby no matter what.

"Of course you must," Charles insisted. "It's illegal not to. You can't go to a quack—I'll tell the police."

"Of course you can," Lisa, her dark-eyed friend at the clothing factory retorted. "If you don't want the baby you'd better get rid of it now, quickly. I'll tell you the name of a doctor who helped me."

"But the money," Ilona wept in anguish. "He'll charge so much."

"Here." The young woman stripped a ring off her finger. "Hock this. You can pay me back a little at a time from your salary."

When Ilona presented herself at the doctor's dingy office and stated her request, he raised his hands in horror. "Never. It is against the law. This is a Catholic country. How dare you ask for such a thing?" He protested loud and long.

"You've done it before," Ilona stated, looking him squarely in the eye. "You helped a friend of mine, and if you don't help me I'll report you to the authorities."

In the face of such blatant blackmail the doctor shrugged and spread his hands. "All right then, come here on Friday. But I warn you that I'm going on vacation the next day, and if there are any complications—" he shrugged again.

"I'll take the risk," Ilona declared.

She never remembered how she got home that Friday afternoon. The ordeal had been far worse than she had expected, and already she shuddered with regrets. She shouldn't have done it. No she shouldn't have—some people said it was murder. Was it? And what if she got an infection—she could be sterile for life. Worse still, what if she died? She'd heard that women sometimes died after these—these "backyard abortions."

By Saturday night Ilona felt as though her whole body was on fire. She tossed and turned, and her delirious ravings so terrified Charles that he sent for Anushka.

Anushka arrived the next morning, and Charles met her at the door.

"She had it," he babbled, "and I think she's going to die. Then the authorities will blame me. But I told her not to. I said—"

Anushka turned away in disgust. Charles seemed less worried about losing his wife than about what would happen to him if she died.

"Go and buy a block of ice," she directed tersely.

As soon as he returned Anushka set to work to reduce her sister's fever with cold compresses.

It took time and a lot of hard work. For several days Anushka wondered whether she would succeed.

Behind their backs the neighbor women whispered to one another. Nobody *knew* but everyone suspected. In ones and twos they came and went, bringing herbal teas and other favorite remedies, helping where they could, each one offering different advice.

Eventually Anushka's selfless ministrations bore fruit. Ilona's fever subsided and her brain cleared. The neighbors bombarded her with beef tea and chicken broth, but by the time she left her bed she was only a ghost of her former self.

"You'd better see a doctor and get a tonic," Anushka advised. "Tell him that you had a miscarriage and lost a lot of blood."

Whether he believed the story or not the doctor at the public-hospital clinic gave no sign. He examined Ilona and prescribed an iron tonic, and as far as they were both concerned the episode ended there.

Except for the abortion and Ilona's consequent three-week-long brush with death the first year of their married life passed like a summer idyll. Charles was the most considerate of husbands, always bringing her gifts and helping her with the heavy housework. He considered that was only fair when she helped earn the money and smiled happily when she thanked him.

Charles stayed home most evenings, and they listened to the radio. On weekends they visited relatives or took long walks into the country. It seemed that all the pessimistic predictions about their chances of happiness had been proved wrong.

Then one Saturday afternoon when Charles was not at home a woman knocked at their door and asked for him. "We work at the

same place," she told Ilona. "So you are Ilona," the woman said.
"I've heard all about you."

"Come in, come in" Ilona invited, delighted to meet one of
Charles's workmates. "Will you take coffee?"

"No." The woman sat down and smoothed her red dress over
her knees. "I may as well tell you," she said avoiding Ilona's
eyes, "Charles wants to divorce you and marry me. I'm pregnant."

"Really?" Ilona sank into a chair opposite her. So Charles
hadn't changed after all. Always, at the back of her mind, she had
expected something like this to happen. What should she say to
this woman?

"This is very awkward because I am pregnant too," she lied,
"and I'm his wife. Now what can we do?"

The woman finally took her leave. When Charles arrived home
Ilona told him about the visitor and what she had said.

"Did she have brown eyes and long dyed blonde hair?" he
asked. When Ilona nodded he said, "Oh, she's a nuisance, that
one. She's got a crush on me and follows me around in the factory. I can't get away from her at all. I'm glad you told her that,
now maybe—"

Ilona only half believed his story, and when the woman appeared again a few months later, she felt sure that Charles was
lying. A year later the same woman took Charles to court, suing
him for maintenance for her and her child. Charles denied it all,
but Ilona found a note hidden in the cuff of his trousers. All it
contained was the woman's name and address, and Ilona decided
to visit her and see the baby for herself.

"She's not at home," the old lady who owned the lodging house
at that address told Ilona. "She's a dreadful woman, that one.
Yes, she's got a baby, three children, in fact, all by different fa-
thers. Got a man for every night of the week, she has."

Of course Charles denied the charges, but evidence piled up
against him. Ilona refused to sleep in the same bed. Charles retali-
ated by refusing to go to work. Just how he spent his days she
never knew, but sometimes she arrived home from work in time to

see furtive looking individuals leaving the apartment. Charles would not say who they were, but he seemed to be always hiding documents or attending meetings.

"It's politics," Ilona told Anushka. "I'm sure that Charles is mixed up with politics."

"Humph," Anushka's snort said as clearly as words. "You should never have married him. I warned you, you should have listened to me."

In 1956 Hungary seethed with unrest. Rumors of revolution and counterrevolution spread through the city. One night Charles rushed into their apartment covered with blood and carrying a pistol.

"What's happened? What have you done?" Ilona leaped from her chair, half hysterical at the sight of blood.

"Shut up." Charles snarled and darted into the kitchen to wash at the sink. "We've got to leave here," he hissed over his shoulder.

"When?"

"As soon as we can. Tomorrow you find out whether any of your family wants to come with us."

"Take only what you can carry in one suitcase," he told Ilona that night. "We'll go ahead. If we get safely through, the others will follow."

But they did not get safely through. Russian soldiers at the border intercepted them, and only the timely arrival of a secret service man known to Charles prevented them both being shipped off to Russia.

"Thank God for that." Safely home again Ilona sighed her relief and went back to work.

In October the revolution began in earnest. In December, just before Christmas, Charles disappeared.

"I'm sure that he is all right," Kati comforted when Ilona went to her and confided her fears. "He's found a way out of Hungary, that's all."

"We're going too," Kati announced a few weeks later when she appeared on Ilona's doorstep with her husband and another man. "We're leaving tomorrow. I'm sorry that we don't have enough money to take you with us."

They all stayed in Ilona's tiny apartment that night, and before she arrived home from work next evening they too had disappeared.

Now Ilona was as alone as she had ever been. Deserted by both husband and sister she lived one day at a time, worrying, wondering, hoping.

One day Ilona's neighbor rapped on her door late at night. "You're wanted on the telephone, I'm sure that it's your husband calling you."

"Charles" Ilona grasped the receiver as if it were a lifeline. "Where are you?"

"I'm in Switzerland. Never mind how I got here; just listen carefully." Then Charles told her to go to a certain address where she would find the wife of a friend of his. "She is coming to Switzerland in a few weeks; you come with her. We'll meet you at the station in Lucerne. Do not fail to do as I say." Charles hung up and left her with a hundred unasked questions trembling on her lips.

"We're slipping out through Yugoslavia," the wife of Charles's friend told Ilona. "You'll have to sell everything you have to get enough money; it's a costly business. Only take as many clothes as you yourself can carry. George wrote me that an old man will guide us across the border. It is dangerous, but he says there are worse places to cross."

Ilona questioned that statement a few weeks later as she huddled in the snow with George's wife and a score of other women and girls, all waiting for the old man who was to guide them into Yugoslavia.

Presently a faint light appeared out of the darkness and a hoarse voice whispered, "Are you ready? Follow me. Don't make a sound."

Scarcely daring to breathe the group followed their leader through the thick trees. On. On. Snow clung to their boots, and the cold infiltrated their heavy clothing. Perhaps it was fear more than the icy wind that made her teeth chatter so. Ilona put a gloved hand to her mouth to muffle the sound.

Suddenly a harsh voice split the frosty stillness.

"Stoy!"

Stoy was one of the few Russian words that Ilona knew, and her heart seemed to stop in obedience to the command. This was it. They'd been caught by the Russians. All these women and girls— they'd be shipped off to Siberia—to a fate worse than death.

"Stoy!"

Ilona caught the dull gleam of lamplight on gun barrel as the old guide shuffled forward to greet the sentry. Then a great wave of relief rippled through the group as word passed back: "It's all right—they just use the same word—we're safe in Yugoslavia."

"Thank God," Ilona said, and in the darkness she hugged George's wife and baby.

Mercifully neither of them foresaw the hardships that lay ahead: the fears and frustration, the endless days of inactivity— herded together like cattle in a pen. The long months in Yugoslavian refugee camps alternating between hope and despair. The separation from George's wife.

Ultimately, through the International Red Cross officials, Ilona received a letter from Charles. It contained a passport and money for her fare. But the money was insufficient.

That was the last straw. The thought of having to spend more endless months in a refugee camp while this affair was straightened out was too much. Alone in a foreign country, understanding scarcely a word that was spoken to her, Ilona broke down and wept.

At the sight of her tears the Swiss consul in whose office the discovery had been made, tut-tutted testily. "Tell her to dry her eyes. I'll pay the difference out of my own pocket."

He stamped her passport with a resounding thud and waved Ilona and her thanks aside.

"Next, please."

When Ilona arrived in Switzerland, she found that Charles had a well-paid position, though what he did to earn his money she did not know. They lived in a fine house in beautiful Lucerne, and for a few months life seemed rosy.

Then George visited them. "How are you getting on? Great place, isn't it? Yes, my wife's fine. Yes, the baby too, growing like a weed." They chatted for a while longer and then George dropped his bombshell.

"We're going to Australia. Oh sure, we love it here. Marvelous scenery, friendly people, but there's no future for us here. Now in Australia—"

They talked for hours. George seemed to have all the needed information on the tip of his tongue. Free passages for persons displaced by war. Language? Yes, of course, totally different from Hungarian, but there were lots of Hungarians already in Australia; besides the government arranged for free language lessons. Jobs? Oh yes, plenty; he spread his arms expansively. Australia's a big place—many times the size of Hungary—and only a small population.

By the time George took his leave Charles had been infected. Ilona sighed. She'd just as soon put her roots down in Switzerland. It wasn't too far from Hungary, and she could at least hope to go back someday and visit her relatives. But Australia! Ilona peered over Charles's shoulder at the atlas he had spread out on the table. Why Australia was away down at the bottom of the world.

Their application for immigration took only a few months to process, and almost before she knew it Charles was prodding her up the gangway and into an old American Army plane. Ilona took one last terrified look at the tarmac and then leaned back in her seat and closed her eyes. She was only thirty-two, too young to die, but if it was God's will—

The long flight finally ended, and Ilona shakily followed her husband out of the plane and into the brilliant Australian sunshine.

New Land—New Life

In after years Ilona preferred to forget the trauma of those first months in Australia. Shunted from one immigration camp to another, trying desperately hard to learn a new language, no work, boredom and unrest among the homesick refugees, disillusionment.

Eventually a Hungarian manager came from Wollongong seeking employees for the huge steel works there. Charles got a job as a turner and fitter but Ilona had to stay behind. There was no place for her in this man's world. Immigrant workers in the steel plant were housed in barracks until they became sufficiently proficient at their jobs and in speaking the language.

"Don't worry," Charles said as he jubilantly took his departure, "I'm sure it won't be for too long."

And it wasn't. A few weeks later Rachel, a Hungarian Jewess who often visited the camp to help the women refugees, learned that Ilona was a seamstress.

"I'll find work for you," she promised. "I know a lot of manufacturers. You leave it to me."

Ilona had no choice, but Rachel kept her word. In a short time she arranged for Ilona's discharge from the camp, introduced her to her workplace, and helped her rent a room in one of Sydney's poorer suburbs.

It wasn't much of a room, small and up three flights of narrow, uncarpeted stairs and it always smelled of gas. Try as she might Ilona never found the leaking pipe; but there were other, worse things to worry about. An occasional rat that scaled the outside drain pipes and entered her room through the open window. And cockroaches! The worn linoleum was cracked and brittle, and at night fat brown cockroaches boldly crawled out and scurried back and forth in search of food. If she kept her foodstuffs in sealed containers they attacked her clothes. Ilona lost underwear and many a pair of hose before she learned.

During the day in the factory perspiration trickled down Ilona's arms and dripped off her elbows as she sewed. Night brought little relief. Cooling breezes seldom found their way through the canyons of tall buildings to stir the tattered lace curtains at her single window.

Closeted in her lonely room Ilona threw herself on the iron bedstead's lumpy mattress and cried for home.

Then came the ultimate misery. Ilona fell ill. Her Australian landlady sent for the only other Hungarian that she knew, a dentist. He came and acted as interpreter between Ilona and the Australian doctor that he brought with him.

"The symptoms indicate that you have stomach ulcers." The doctor looked sympathetically at Ilona. "I think you'd better go to the hospital for a while."

"Never!" Ilona burst into tears. Between them the two men and the landlady persuaded her that it would be best. While the landlady packed some clothing for her to take with her, the dentist offered to let Charles know what had happened.

To Ilona's surprise Charles took a day off work and made the eighty-three kilometer train journey to visit her.

"This is no good," Charles said as he kissed her on both cheeks. "We can't go on like this. You must come down to Wollongong. We'll find a way."

"It wouldn't be so bad if I could speak the language properly." Tears slid down Ilona's pale cheeks. "The nurses are kind, but I can't talk to them."

Two days later Charles visited her again. He beamed as he produced an estate agent's brochure for her perusal. "I've found a house for rent. It's expensive but I've worked out how we can afford it."

"How?" Ilona smiled. The prospect of settling down somewhere made her feel better already.

Charles smiled. "There are many Hungarian men working in
the Wollongong district, most of them alone. They get so tired of
Australian food. Fish and chips, and meat pies with tomato
sauce." His lips curled in distaste. "They would pay anything for
a goulash or a *tolt ott kaposzta* like you make, Illona."

"Now if we rented this big house we could let out some of the
rooms, have some of these men stay with us, 'boarding' it's called
in Australia. Then you need not go out sewing; just stay at home
and cook their meals."

"Do you really think that would work out all right?"

"Of course. You're a fine cook. You know that."

"Well, we'll try." Ilona smiled. As soon as she left the hospital
she gave notice to her landlady and the manager of the clothing
factory.

"Moving down to Wollongong, are you?" Rachel mused when
she heard of Ilona's plans. "My brother-in-law works in a steel
mill down that way. You may meet him sometime."

The boarding establishment filled rapidly as the fame of Ilona's
cooking spread.

"Nagyon jo, nagyon jo," the men said and smacked their lips
and passed back their plates for more.

But all too soon Ilona found that boarding hungry Hungarians
was not a paying proposition at all. Her generous heart could not
bear to cut corners. She used the best, the most expensive ingredi-
ents for her *turos teszta* and all her other excellent Hungarian
dishes—and as a consequence she did not help to pay the rent; she
lost money on the deal.

"This won't do," Charles stormed at her.

She did try to cut corners, but it was no use.

After a few months trial Ilona gave up her boardinghouse and
went back to sewing. The Sydney manufacturer agreed to her doing sewing at home, so every Monday she took the train to Sydney
and carried two heavy suitcases of cut garments back to

Wollongong to be stitched. Every Friday she returned to Sydney with the completed garments. She sewed quickly and neatly and even on piecework she soon earned enough money to purchase a sewing machine of her own. Charles earned good money at his work. Little by little their bank account grew.

Their first year in Australia drew to a close. Then early in the new year a letter came from Kati in London asking whether they would help her and her husband immigrate to Australia.

"Of course," Ilona wrote back, "we have a big house; there is plenty of room and plenty of work in this district. We'll be glad to see you soon."

But Kati and her husband did not like the dirty city with its huge mills and mines and factories. At their urging Charles gave up his job, and the four of them moved to Sydney. Work was easy enough to come by, and for a while the four all shared another large house.

But that did not work out either. Long before, Kati had given up her ideas about religion. She and her husband fought like the proverbial Kilkenny cats. Charles took the husband's side, so that made Kati hate him too. Ilona took her sister's part against both men, and the resulting shouting matches sent the neighbors scurrying—some to close their windows and others to listen behind drawn shades.

"I wish I'd never met him at all," Kati sobbed to her sister when the two of them were alone. "Marriage is nothing like I thought it would be. Papa and Mama never quarrelled. I thought it would be like that, but we can't agree on *anything*. I hate him, I wish—"

Ilona nodded in sober agreement. "Me too. I wish I'd listened to Anushka. I'd be much better off alone. I can see now that I never loved Charles. I was flattered by his attentions, that's all. And then he tried to kill me, and I was too terrified not to marry him." She wiped her eyes and managed a weak smile. "At least in this country he is faithful to me."

"Faithful?" Kati sneered. "That's only because he hasn't had opportunity to be otherwise." She stopped short and then added half to herself, "Maybe we'd both be better off if we'd stayed with the church."

After the next big row Charles and Ilona found a small apartment in an adjoining suburb. They moved out and left Kati and her husband to solve their own marital problems.

Ilona and Charles worked hard all day and rarely went out at night. There was no money to spare for entertainment. Several evenings each week another of Ilona's Jewish-Hungarian friends visited, and the three of them played cards. Hannah's husband had done well in Australia, but his prosperous business necessitated a lot of travel and Hannah was often alone.

Hannah was not short of money. She had her own car, and she always wore enough jewelry to make Ilona envious. But she was pleasant company, and Ilona never forgot her early kindnesses.

Charles enjoyed Hannah's company too. But to what extent, Ilona had no idea until she came home from work one evening to find a note propped up against the flower vase in the center of the table. She scarcely had time to digest its message before the telephone rang. It was Hannah's husband and he was furious.

"Didn't you know? You didn't even suspect? Pshaw! How could anyone be so blind? You were on the spot. They've gone to Brisbane, you know. Bah, let them be. She'll come crawling back when the money runs out."

After the initial shock Ilona accepted Charles's absence with philosophic calm. "Better no apple at all than a bad one," she told Kati. "He'll come crawling back when she tires of him. But I won't forgive him this time."

Sure enough Charles came back. Several months later Ilona arrived home from work to find him waiting at the door.

"I'm sorry," he said. "I—"

"I'm not." Ilona looked him full in the face. "I'm glad. Take the rest of your things that you left here and get out. I never want to see you again."

For months Charles kept coming back and trying to placate Ilona but this time she remained adamant. For the first time in years she felt completely happy. So happy, in fact, that she decided to visit Marishka, an old friend from boardinghouse days, and tell her all about it.

"I feel as if a great weight has been lifted off my back, Marishka. He was never faithful to me, never," Ilona confided.

"Ach, you need someone like Gyula." Marishka clicked her tongue in admiration. "Such a fine man. Honest and hard-working. Ah, if only I were twenty years younger."

"Who is Gyula?" Ilona smiled at her old friend's description. The two women sat in Marishka's kitchen and shelled peas while they visited. Whenever she could wangle a day off from work Ilona caught the train to Wollongong to see Marishka, the Hungarian woman who had helped and befriended her when she and Charles had first come to Wollongong.

"He is one of my boarders." Marishka clicked her tongue again. "So kind, Ilona, so gentle and quiet. While the other men are guzzling beer at the hotel he sits here and reads the newspaper to improve his English. He's not married either." She cast a sidelong glance at Ilona. "Not married, Ilona, and about your age."

"He sounds too perfect." Ilona sighed and gathered up the peapods. "I don't think I'm interested in any more men, Marishka. One mistake is enough."

"Ach, but Gyula—"

Ilona shook her head and then looked at her watch. "I must rush, Marishka, or I'll miss my train." She picked up her coat and handbag and kissed her old friend good-bye.

"Come again," Marishka hugged her tightly. "Come as often as you can."

Ilona's next visit to Wollongong coincided with a public holiday. She did not have to hurry back to work, but could spend the night in Marishka's spotless spareroom and return to Sydney the following day. Now, also, she would meet this wonderful Gyula that Marishka talked so much about. Despite her protestations otherwise, Ilona's feminine curiosity had been aroused.

"Ilona, this is Gyula; Gyula, this is Ilona, my friend from Sydney."

Ilona looked up into expressive brown eyes that smiled down at her and seemed to say, "So you're the girl I've heard so much about."

"How do you do?" Ilona extended her hand in proper Australian fashion, but she felt herself blushing under Gyula's steady gaze.

"How do *you* do?" He returned, and his hand held hers for a second longer than necessary.

Ilona's heart skipped a beat. Confused thoughts tumbled about in her mind. Was it possible? Could one fall in love at first sight? Surely not at thirty-five?

The blood pounded in her ears as Gyula still stood there quietly looking down at her. She only half heard Marishka chattering on.

"Ach! I'm getting so forgetful—there's nothing in the house to drink, and those men will all be in soon, all with thirsts like desert camels. Ilona, please go to the corner shop and buy some drinks; lemonade, anything will do. Gyula, you must go with her to help her carry them."

It was all so obvious, so very, very obvious that Ilona felt her color rise again. Gyula smiled at her. His eyes twinkled and his kind voice said, "Come, Ilona, we have a lot of talking to do."

Marishka had done her work well. Before Ilona and Gyula returned from their errand at the shop Ilona had discovered that the attraction was mutual. Not only that, but they agreed on everything they discussed; and their background was so similar. Both had been reared on the outskirts of beautiful Budapest, now both refugees from tragic Hungary endeavoring to build a new life in a new land.

"You must call me John," Gyula said. "That's what the Australians call me. This is my country now; it has given me so much." He looked at Ilona in a way that made her smile in undiluted happiness.

Little wonder that from then on Ilona siezed every opportunity to visit Wollongong.

For his part John suddenly found Sydney very attractive. He arranged his work shift so that once or twice a week he worked all night at the steel mill and then in the morning changed his clothes and dozed in the train on the way to Sydney to spend as many of the daylight hours as possible with his beloved.

So two years passed. Not trouble-free years, for Charles gave Ilona no peace. Every few months he appeared at her door. "Do you like my new suit? Come and see the television that I have purchased."

"I don't care what you wear or what you buy or what you do," Ilona told him again and again. "I don't want to see you. You are not part of my life anymore."

"You've found someone else," Charles accused. "I know there's a fellow visiting you."

"Yes, I have," Ilona threw back. "God has sent me a good man, not one like—" She left the sentence unfinished and closed the door.

Eventually John gave up his Wollongong job and moved to Sydney to work at his old trade of motor mechanic. He boarded with his brother and sister-in-law and to get away from Charles, Ilona moved in with Kati and her husband.

"Yes, Gyula," Ilona said when John asked her to marry him. When they were alone they often lapsed into their mother tongue. It seemed a more natural medium for the tender things that they wanted to say to each other.

"There's just one thing," John continued and Ilona caught her breath. What is it? Hadn't he told her all his past? She had been honest with him. What—?

Gyula took her hand in his and looked into her eyes. "Ilona, if you will marry me I will do everything I can to make you happy. In return I ask but one thing."

"What is it, Gyula?" Ilona scarcely whispered the words.

John smiled broadly, "I want you always to cook the best food—feed me well, Ilona. I have known hunger—starvation." His eyes darkened, and Ilona knew that cruel memories of his years in prison camp had come back to haunt him. He always looked like that when he talked about the years in Russia. "I will earn the money, Ilona, and you make the good food. Feed me well, my darling!''

"Yes, Gyula.'' Ilona threw her arms around his neck. She would try and make up to him for all those terrible years. She promised to feed him well.

Two more years passed before they could be married. Charles resisted every suggestion of divorce. Repeatedly he tried to bring about a reconciliation. When that failed he adopted his former attitude of, "If I can't have you, no one else shall." Even after Ilona initiated divorce proceedings he did his utmost to hinder the case.

Eventually everything was settled and Ilona and John were married in September 1964. Using their combined savings they paid a deposit on a city service station and then set to work to pay off the balance.

They worked ten, and sometimes more, hours a day for seven days a week. They took no time off, no holidays. While John cared for the vehicle repairs Ilona served at the petrol pumps. Her soft hands became hard and callused like a workingman's hands.

But she did not forget her promise to John. There was no time to go home to their small apartment to prepare meals, so she had a small stove and a sink installed at the back of the service station. In between serving customers she prepared and cooked their meals—and such meals. Regular customers who called for service around mealtimes, sniffed, and asked, "What are you cooking, Ilona? It smells delicious.''

Soul Food

A dozen happy years passed. Kati and her husband still resided in Sydney, and the two couples frequently exchanged visits. One evening while the husbands discussed business matters in the living room, the two sisters bustled around in Kati's kitchen preparing supper.

Suddenly Kati looked up from the onions she was slicing and announced, "I'm going back to church, Ilona."

"What did you say?" Ilona asked. Her startled ears could not take in the full import of the words. Church? Kati hadn't mentioned church in years.

"I'm going back to church," Kati repeated slowly. "Why don't you come with me?"

"Why are you going now? What will your husband say?"

"I don't know, but I must go." Kati took a step toward her sister and said solemnly. "For years God's Spirit has been calling me, but I have not listened. If I keep on ignoring His voice He will cease to call; then I shall have committed the unpardonable sin." Her voice sank to a whisper that terrified Ilona.

"The unpardonable sin?" Ilona repeated.

"Come with me, Ilona. I've found out that there is a Seventh-day Adventist Church at Woollahra not far from here."

"I can't. You know that I can't." Ilona protested through dry lips. "We work every day of the week; it is impossible."

"I don't like to go alone," Kati protested, "please come with me."

Ilona shook her head.

Kati attended the church alone, and the next day she telephoned her sister. "Oh, it was wonderful," she bubbled. "Just like the old days back on Szecej Bertilan Ucca. They are such friendly people, so warm and loving, just the same as they were back in Budapest. You must come, Ilona, you must."

"I can't," Ilona reiterated. "You know that I can't."

For a whole year Kati attended church alone. Then she changed her tactics.

"All right," she said when Ilona once again refused her invitation. "If you won't come with me I won't go anymore."

"But you must go." Ilona's voice echoed her alarm. Visions of her sister committing the unpardonable sin flashed through her mind.

"No, if you won't come with me I won't go."

"But I have to work every day. We only close the service station once a year, on Christmas Day."

"Then come to church on Christmas Day," Kati made no effort to hide her jubilation. "It falls on Saturday this year."

John offered no objection when Ilona suggested that they go to Kati's church on Christmas Day. During the years since their marriage she had often talked to him about the Seventh-day Adventist Church, and though he did not share her interest in religion he held no prejudices.

"In fact," his brown eyes twinkled down at her, "it might do me some good."

So on Christmas Day 1976 Kati and her husband and Ilona and John Nagy joined the Woollahra Seventh-day Adventist church members who were worshiping as usual on the Sabbath day.

The years fell away as Ilona listened to the hymns and the lesson study and the service. Once again she was a little girl sitting beside Kati in the Szecej Bertilan Ucca Church. Once again she was hearing about the second coming of Jesus. Ah yes, of course, Christmas, noel, celebrated His *first* coming—to Bethlehem's manger.

He would come again, the *second* coming, to take His righteous people home to heaven. Oh, how she wished—

"Ilona," John said one evening as she washed the supper dishes and he dried them, "Why don't we sell the garage?"

"Sell the garage?" Ilona's astonished eyes opened as wide as her gasping mouth. But before she could give an opinion John continued.

"I've been thinking a lot about it. Our new house is all paid for." His eyes rested appreciatively on the comfortable furnishings of their modern house.

"My chest is troubling me a lot lately. Yes, yes, I know I'm going on fifty-two; but why should we work ourselves to death? Let's sell and take a trip back home."

"Home?" Ilona's excited reaction made John laugh. "See everyone again?" That is, she added to herself, everyone that is left in Hungary. Distance and death had separated most of the brothers and sisters and their families.

"That would be wonderful." Ilona scurried around the kitchen and finished the chores in record time; then they sat down to make their plans.

Within a few short months all arrangements had been made and the Nagys were on their way. The trip proved to be all that Ilona had anticipated. Excited reunion with Anushka and her husband, and as many of their children and grandchildren as could be mustered for the occasion; re-meeting brothers and sisters-in-law and sisters and brothers-in-law, nieces, nephews, and their children; reunion with Susie. Darling Susie, she hadn't altered much, only grown older.

"Like me—like me too!" Ilona ran her hands over her own gray-streaked fair hair and the crow's feet at the corners of her eyes. "Such a long time since we've seen each other, *Zsuzsi*. Do you remember—?"

Even stolid John's smile stretched ear to ear as he visited his old haunts in Budapest. Many things had improved; many other things had not changed at all. The market scarcely altered after twenty years, with Andras returned to Hungary and now a prosperous, middle-aged stall-owner. Papa and Mama had gone to their rest, of course, but Istvan was still there and still driving trucks; little sister Mariska had long before emigrated and married a Canadian.

All too soon the holiday ended, and Ilona and John returned to Australia with happy memories enough to last them the rest of their lives. Their friends and relatives welcomed them back, the weather displayed its most glorious blue and white skies and golden sunshine, and within a few days life resumed its normal tenor.

John easily found work as a motor mechanic at a nearby garage. When friends teased and told him that he'd slipped down in the world, he laughed slyly as he said, "What does it matter? I only work five days a week now, instead of seven; and only eight hours a day, instead of twelve. The pay is good—and the boss has all the headaches."

Now that Ilona had no garage work responsibilities her cooking and home-making talents rose to dizzying heights. The aromas of Ilona's goulashes and *makos tesztas* tantalized neighborhood noses. The windows of the Nagy's house shone cleaner than any others in the suburb. Not a speck of dust dared to linger on the shining surfaces of their furniture and fittings. While John looked on and smiled indulgently, his impulsive little wife filled their childless home with all the beautiful things that early poverty had denied them both: fine bone china, exquisite needlework, oil paintings, and copper etchings.

Kati often visited Ilona and admired the purchases she made. But not long after their return from abroad she had again broached the subject of church attendance.

"You don't have to work on Saturdays now, Ilona. Why don't you come with me? I want you to meet Rudy Iro too. He's taking the theology course at Avondale College and—"

Finally Ilona accompanied Kati to church, and Rudy and his wife and three little boys entered the Nagy's life. Though they might now all be naturalized Australians they were still Hungarians at heart and liked nothing better than to visit together and eat Hungarian food and talk about home. Whenever he could spare the time from college Rudy visited and lost no opportunity of telling Ilona and John about his heavenly home and his heavenly Father.

For nearly a year Ilona continued to attend church on her own. Not that she ever felt lonely. She was part of a big family, and the church members were her new sisters and brothers.

On one or two special occasions John accompanied her to church. Not because religion interested him but to silence her importunings. Given the slightest opportunity she talked to him about Jesus—His soon return, the way He had guided in her life, His answers to her prayers, His constant love in spite of her years of neglect.

John listened with a tolerant ear. When she finished her passionate explanations of the signs of Christ's coming listed in Matthew 24 or related Revelation's prophecies of the event, he nodded politely.

Then in 1979 the minister of the Woollahra Seventh-day Adventist church announced that he intended to have illustrated Bible lectures on Monday nights in a suburban hall.

Illustrated Bible lectures. Would John like that? Ilona wondered. She would ask him to attend. He could only say No.

But John did not say No. He went along quite willingly, and as far as Ilona could tell he enjoyed the pictures and the lecture. Except for his wheezing cough he sat silent and attentive. Several times he nodded his head in agreement with what the minister said.

John handled the English language more expertly than Ilona did, and on their way home afterward he explained some of the finer points of the lecture to her.

"Archeology—that means digging up old cities that have been buried for thousands of years—proves that the Bible is true. That is what he was talking about tonight. That is why he showed pictures of Babylon's deserted ruins. He—"

As she listened Ilona clenched her teeth to prevent herself rejoicing out loud, but in her heart she exulted, "Lord, he liked it. He listened. Win his heart, Lord, he must follow You. John must be ready for Your coming. He must."

John continued to attend the Monday-night lectures with Ilona. A few weeks later the minister's assistant called at their home. John welcomed him inside and bombarded him with questions. Then the minister himself came and arranged to have Bible studies with them.

Week by week John's interest increased, and so did Ilona's excitement. She had never attended an evangelistic series herself or taken a course of Bible studies. She had no background of biblical knowledge other than the memory of those long ago Sabbaths when she was a child in Budapest. And now this—this—it exceeded her wildest expectations.

"It's wonderful, isn't it, John?" she rejoiced one night after the minister left. "Isn't it just marvelous how the Lord has led us?"

"Yes, my dear," John smiled and took her hand in his. "I can see it all so plainly now. All my life I have been burdened with chest problems; I survived several serious illnesses; for more than two years I starved in a prisoner of war camp—but God miraculously preserved me because He wanted to give me eternal life.

"And you," he smiled into her eyes, "little did I know when you promised to feed me well, Ilona, that one day you would introduce me to the best food of all, the Bread of Life."

John and Ilona Nagy were baptized into the Seventh-day Adventist church on December 19, 1981. In the whole of Australia it would be hard to find a happier couple. Reaching for the well-worn Bible that had once belonged to Ilona's mother, John turned to the Gospel of John, chapter 6. "And Jesus said unto them, I am the bread of life: he that cometh to me shall never hunger.

"I am the living bread which came down from heaven: if any man eat of this bread, he shall live for ever: and the bread that I will give is my flesh, which I will give for the life of the world." Verses 35 and 51. Then looking over at his wife, he smiles as he says, "Ah, yes, Ilona, you *have* fed me well, my darling."